SOCIALISM SUCKS

"What a captivating idea *Socialism Sucks* embraces! A worldwide tour guide written in plain English by two high-end economists. An invasion of the world's most highly regulated hot spots where they can't even efficiently produce or distribute something as simple and lovable as beer. A down-to-earth, almost fable-like lesson showing socialism's failures for all the world to see. And it even has some sidesplitting hilarity thrown in. I knew these guys were great; but I didn't know this side of them. Buy this book. Give it to your children and grandchildren, and to anyone who touts the nonsense—now fashionable in some American circles—that government power somehow produces more happiness than personal liberty."

> **—JUDGE ANDREW P. NAPOLITANO**, senior judicial analyst for
> Fox News

"Every country that enters socialism gets more miserable; every country that leaves it prospers: that's the lesson of history so far. Robert Lawson's and Ben Powell's light-hearted book drives home this message in a refreshingly readable way. From Venezuela's immiseration to Georgia's liberation, the authors sample every socialist, ex-socialist, semi-socialist and supposedly socialist experiment, beer by beer."

> **—MATT RIDLEY**, author of *The Evolution of Everything*

"Professors Robert Lawson and Benjamin Powell do a yeomen's job in proving that socialism sucks, the apt title for their new book. They show why there's no stampede into countries like Venezuela and Cuba and other socialist darlings of the U.S. leftists. What's more, over a couple of drinks, Lawson and Powell prove that Sweden is not as socialistic as portrayed by our leftists."

> **—WALTER E. WILLIAMS**, professor of economics,
> George Mason University

"In theory, socialism sucks and economists know why. Here are two economists who ventured far beyond the ivory tower to discover that in practice, the theory is right. This is the tragic story of mass suffering in the name of an insane idea, told with sympathy, insight, and no small amount of black humor. Read it and weep; read it and laugh; read it and learn."

—**STEVEN LANDSBURG**, professor of economics, University of Rochester, and author of the *Armchair Economist*

"What is 'socialism'? And do countries that overindulge in it wake up with bad hangovers? You bet they do. Robert Lawson and Benjamin Powell give you the hair-of-the-dog cure. They provide a dose of political economy knowledge mixed with an understanding of the benefits of economic freedom, add a strong dash of humor, and top it off with a cold beer. Have a Bob & Ben Eye-Opener and you'll feel like (and live in a place where you can make) a million dollars!"

—**P. J. O'ROURKE**, author of #1 *New York Times* bestseller *Parliament of Whores* and *Holidays in Hell*

SOCIALISM SUCKS

SOCIALISM SUCKS

SUCKS

TWO ECONOMISTS DRINK THEIR WAY THROUGH THE UNFREE WORLD

ROBERT LAWSON AND BENJAMIN POWELL

REGNERY PUBLISHING
A Division of Salem Media Group

Regnery® is a registered trademark of Salem Communications Holding Corporation

Cataloging-in-Publication data on file with the Library of Congress

ISBN 978-1-62157-945-8
ebook ISBN 978-1-62157-946-5

Published in the United States by
Regnery Publishing
A Division of Salem Media Group
300 New Jersey Ave NW
Washington, DC 20001
www.Regnery.com

Manufactured in the United States of America

10 9 8 7 6 5 4 3 2 1

Books are available in quantity for promotional or premium use. For information on discounts and terms, please visit our website: www.Regnery.com.

For Tracy, Lisa, Keri & Raymond
In appreciation for your patience with our travels

CONTENTS

FOREWORD

I n 2013, Venezuela was the poster child for socialism.

It was the standard against which celebrities and politicos alike measured the United States' economy, which they found wanting.

At Salon, David Sirota let us know that yes, this was socialism, and yes, it should incite envy in Americans. Venezuelan president Hugo Chávez, said Sirota, with his "full-throated advocacy of socialism," had "racked up an economic record that ... American president[s] could only dream of achieving."

Fashionable opinion couldn't say enough about Venezuela and its president. Sean Penn, Danny Glover, Oliver Stone, and Michael Moore were the tip of the iceberg.

And then, by 2017, Venezuela—the very country these commentators had been lecturing everyone about, and which Sirota had praised for its "full-throated advocacy of socialism"—suddenly became *not real socialism*, even though nothing about it had changed.

Well, I guess at least one thing changed: by 2016 nearly three out of four Venezuelans lacked a diet that researchers considered optimal (that's a generous way of putting it), and nearly 16 percent had resorted to eating garbage.

Oh, we don't want Venezuela, say our "democratic socialists" today. Why, we want Sweden!

This kind of claim might be more believable had so many of the people making it not cheered Venezuela right up to the moment that starvation and chaos were everywhere.

There's plenty to say regarding Sweden: (1) its "socialist" policies were made possible by wealth created under an essentially capitalist economy (as recently as the 1950s, remember, government spent less as a percentage of GDP in Sweden than in the U.S.); (2) Swedes earn about 50 percent more in the U.S., in our supposedly wicked economy; and (3) since Sweden's explosion of social welfare spending there have been zero jobs created on net in the private sector.

No, thanks.

In recent years, sympathy for socialism in the U.S. has grown rapidly. No doubt one reason was the financial crisis of 2008. Critics felt certain that this episode revealed a profound sickness at the heart of American capitalism. Yet the crisis would certainly not have happened without the twin evils of government policy and Federal Reserve intervention, both of which are something like the opposite of capitalism.

And there's another, more fundamental reason: it's an easy argument to follow. (1) Those people over there have lots of money. (2) You would like some money. (3) We are happy to facilitate the transfer.

"The rich," meanwhile, are caricatured and despised as a matter of routine. And while it's true that some people have come by their wealth in disreputable ways, made possible by government, socialist critics are not making fine distinctions like this. It is wealth per se, no matter how acquired, that is to be condemned.

Not a moment's thought is applied to wondering what the rich might actually do for the economy. We are to believe that they roll around in their cash until it sticks to their sweaty bodies.

Not a word about investment in capital goods, which make the economy more physically productive and increase real incomes. Nothing about capital maintenance, which keeps the structure of production up and running. Nothing about saving at all, since most popular critics of capitalism appear to think consumption is what really contributes to economic health—as if simply using things up could make us rich.

From this standpoint, socialism seems to make sense. There are no unintended consequences of government intervention worth thinking about. We have rich people over there, and things we'd like to do with their money over here, so what's the problem? If there's an outcome we want, why, we simply legislate it into existence! Want higher wages? Just pass a law!

If this were true, poverty could have been conquered anytime, anywhere. We ought to call the folks in Bangladesh and let them know: poverty is over! You just need to pass some laws!

Now were we to impose the American regulatory apparatus, and American labor laws and wage requirements, on Bangladesh, virtually the entire country would become instantly unemployable and poverty would only intensify.

It's almost as if there's something other than regulation and redistribution that accounts for economic progress.

Among the great merits of *Socialism Sucks* are that it's short, engaging, and easily digested—which is precisely what the anti-socialist, pro-freedom side needs right now.

Your guides on the tour of the unfree world you are about to embark upon could scarcely be better chosen, I might add. Bob Lawson, who has done extensive research on the economic freedom of the various countries of the world, has important insight into what works and what doesn't. Ben Powell's book on sweatshops, published by Cambridge University Press, explains what needs to be done (and what needs to be avoided) for the developing world to prosper—as well as the various ways that ignorant, if sometimes well-intentioned, Westerners retard that process.

Turn the page, and your journey begins. The good news: when it's all done, you can close the book and be back in semi-capitalist America.

At least for now, that is.

Tom Woods
TomsPodcast.com

NOT SOCIALISM: SWEDEN

SEPTEMBER 2009

"If I've got one major bitch about Sweden," I said as I sat across the table from Bob at the Duvel Café in Stockholm, "it's the alcohol prices."

The Duvel Café isn't a dive, but it's not a swanky, high-end bar either. Behind its plain, black, street-front exterior is a five-seat bar with high-alcohol Belgian beers on tap, a few booths, and the uncomfortable wooden window seat that was causing a major pain in my ass. Yet, despite the relative geographic proximity to Belgium, our Belgian beers cost far more than what we were accustomed to paying in the U.S.

"Fucking taxes," he answered. "Sweden has to pay for its welfare state." He was right. Sweden taxes alcohol at rates higher than most countries. In fact, Sweden taxes everything. A lot.

Sweden is the first stop on our tour of socialist countries, even though it's not a socialist country. Wait. What? You heard Sweden was an example of how socialism works? Though lots of people believe Sweden is a socialist country, and some of our politicians try to use that misunderstanding to advance their own agendas, we're going to present evidence to the contrary. But first, let me give you a little background about Bob and me, so you'll know where we're coming from.

Bob grew up in Cincinnati, Ohio. His background is working-class, and he's a lifelong fan of Cincinnati's subpar professional sports teams. While earning his PhD at Florida State University in the early 1990s, Bob became involved in a project analyzing quantitative data that would finally settle a question that has long been a point of disagreement among social scientists: whether a more capitalist government or a more socialist government creates conditions that translate to a better quality of life for its citizens.

The idea for Bob's economic freedom index, published in the Fraser Institute's annual *Economic Freedom of the World* report, started with Milton Friedman, the Nobel Prize–winning economist, and Michael Walker, the executive director of the Fraser Institute in Vancouver. Since the mid-1990s, Bob has worked with Professor James Gwartney of Florida State to put out the Fraser Institute's annual economic freedom index. We'll talk about the index a lot in this book. Bob was a professor at Shawnee State and Capital University, both in Ohio, and Auburn University in Alabama, before he landed his current gig in Dallas where he is the director of the O'Neil Center for Global Markets and Freedom at the Cox School of Business at Southern Methodist University.

I come from a similar working-class background in Haverhill, Massachusetts, about thirty miles north of Boston, and remain an avid fan of Boston's decidedly superior sports franchises. Our differing allegiances don't hurt our friendship. In fact, Bob's a loyal enough fan of his Bengals to bet me a bottle of liquor, without the benefit of a spread, each time they play the Patriots. I've enjoyed drinking those bottles, though I suspect he's regifting me the booze he's won from another friend of his who insists on rooting for the Browns.

I earned my PhD at George Mason University and went on to be a professor at San Jose State University in California and Suffolk University in Boston before taking a position as an economics professor and director of the Free Market Institute at Texas Tech University six years ago.

Bob and I became friends at a Mont Pelerin Society meeting in Salt Lake City in 2004. The economist Friedrich Hayek founded the society in Mont Pelerin, Switzerland, in 1947, bringing together accomplished academics from around the world concerned with the spread of socialism and totalitarianism. Over the years, eight members of the Mont Pelerin Society have won Nobel Prizes, including Hayek and Friedman. Today, the society has more than five hundred members—not just academics, but business, political, and intellectual leaders—who share a commitment to defending freedom.

Salt Lake City was dry back in 2004, except for "private clubs," essentially bars that sold short-term memberships as a cover charge. Bob and I became members and drinking companions at one such club near our hotel, and we climbed our first mountain together in the nearby Wasatch Range. We've since shared countless drinks, attended dozens of economics conferences, and climbed many mountains.

Bob and I also share a devotion to freedom and free markets. But our devotion is not mere ideology, it is also informed by economic theory and evidence. Nobel prize–winning economist James

Buchanan believed understanding economic principles allows "the average man … to command the heights of genius," but that without these principles "he is a jibbering idiot."[1] In many ways we're fairly regular guys, but our training in economic theory and our analysis of economic data allow us to see, understand, and explain the world a little differently than most people—and, we hope, help us to avoid being "jibbering idiots."

This book is a truthful accounting of our travels, and so includes our sometimes excessive drinking, low-grade misogyny, and salty language. We are white, middle-aged, American males who are not "woke" and don't even know what "intersectionality" means. If that offends you, you can put this book down and read one of our boring academic journal articles instead. It will make the same points but without the local color.

In this book, though, we're aiming for a popular audience that will appreciate not just our economic insights but our down-to-earth honesty. We wrote this book because too many people seem to be dangerously ignorant of what socialism is, how it functions, and its historical track record. We also wanted to get drunk in Cuba, and this was a great way to write off our expenses.

* * *

In the spring of 2016, a Harvard survey found that a third of eighteen- to twenty-nine-year-olds supported socialism.[2] Another survey, from the Victims of Communism Memorial Foundation, reported that millennials supported socialism over any other economic system.[3]

The Young Democratic Socialists of America, which had only twelve chapters on college campuses at the end of 2016, burgeoned to nearly fifty chapters by fall 2017.[4] Twenty-year-old Michelle Fisher, the national co-chair of the organization, said, "I think people in my generation—people who grew up post-Cold War—I don't think socialism is as much a scarlet S as it is for older folks.... The taboo for me was never there."[5]

Obviously not. The Victims of Communism survey found that 31 percent of millennials had a favorable view of Che Guevara; 23 percent thought well of Vladimir Lenin; and 19 percent approved of Mao Zedong, so at least two out of ten millennials apparently think that mass murder in the interest of socialism isn't so bad. That's one of the taboos that's fallen.

But it isn't just young people who ignore or deny socialism's pernicious past. In 2017, the *New York Times* ran a weekly column, "Red Century: Exploring the history and legacy of Communism, 100 years after the Russian Revolution."[6] While the columnists and topics varied from week to week, there was little focus on the intentional mass killings carried out by socialist regimes. Nor was there much mention of the economic insanity of socialist governments that resulted in millions of people starving to death. In an entire year's worth of columns, only one discussed how socialism led to economic stagnation. Overwhelmingly, the *Times* treated us to columns about how socialism was merely an advanced form of liberalism, highlighting the allegedly green policies of "Lenin's Eco-Warriors" and instructing us on "Why Women Had Better Sex Under Socialism."

At about the same time, Bernie Sanders, a self-proclaimed democratic socialist, made a strong run for the Democratic Party nomination for president, getting 43 percent of the vote in the 2016 Democratic primaries.

How can so many Americans view socialism so favorably, when in practice it has led to misery and mass murder? The answer is that, like the *New York Times*, many people assume that socialism is merely a more generous form of liberalism.

The Victims of Communism survey found that only a third of millennials could define socialism correctly. In the first Democratic Party debate, Sanders was asked how a socialist could win a general election in the United States. He pointed to "countries like Denmark, like Sweden and Norway," as examples of his version of socialism.[7] But those countries aren't socialist.

Sweden does have a big welfare state, government-provided health care, and generous unemployment benefits, and the drinks at Duvel Café were indeed highly taxed. But welfare and entitlement programs, however highly prized by socialism's acolytes, are not the defining components of socialism.

The economic freedom index that Bob helped create is probably the best way to measure whether a country has a more capitalist or socialist system. The index uses a zero-to-ten scale, with higher scores indicating a more capitalist system. If a country earns a high score on the index, that generally means that country keeps government taxation low, respects private property rights, maintains the value of its currency, lets people trade freely, and keeps regulations to a minimum.

So how does Sweden stack up? Overall, Sweden gets a 7.54 rating, which is good enough for twenty-seventh place out of the 159 countries in the study. Sure, Sweden taxes the bejesus out of its citizens. Its tax-and-spend score is very low indeed—3.64 out of 10. It regulates labor markets quite a lot (6.81) as well, but overall it does a good job protecting property rights (8.35), avoiding inflation (9.71), allowing free trade (8.28), and only lightly regulating credit markets (9.90) and businesses more generally (8.08). Of the other Nordic countries Comrade Bernie mentioned, Denmark rates 8.0 and Norway 7.62. All three rank in the top fifth of the most economically free countries in the world.

Bottom line: Sweden is a prosperous, mostly capitalist country. When we were there we could see this with our own eyes. The Swedes were obviously wealthy, their buildings were well maintained, and their beer was good and cold. In fact, what we saw was consistent with the research that uses the economic freedom index to measure the impact of economic freedom on living standards. In a recent review of nearly two hundred academic studies, Bob and his co-author Joshua Hall concluded, "Over two-thirds of these studies found economic freedom to correspond to a 'good' outcome such as faster growth, better living standards, more happiness, etc. Less than four percent of the sample found economic freedom to be associated with a 'bad' outcome such as increased income inequality."[8]

Although Sweden is still mostly free today, it used to be even freer. Our Swedish friend, Johan Norberg, has told the story of how laissez-faire economic reforms made Sweden rich.[9] In his telling, back in the early 1860s his ancestors were so poor that they had to mix tree bark into their bread recipe when they were short on flour. Incomes in Sweden at that time were on par with those in the Congo today. Meanwhile, life expectancies were half as long and infant mortality rates three times as high as they are in many modern poor countries.

But nineteenth-century economic reformers liberalized Sweden's economy and created a prosperous, capitalist country. Our personal favorite reformer, Lars Johan Hierta, is honored with a copper statue about a kilometer from the Duvel Café. We like Lars because he championed free speech, equal rights for women, business freedom, free trade, small government, and the repeal of public drunkenness laws (as long as the drunk didn't threaten anyone). Cheers to that!

Ben and Bob, along with fellow economist Brad Hobbs, enjoy some excellent but highly taxed Belgian beer in Sweden.

Hierta and other reformers eventually implemented many of their policies, and Sweden grew rapidly. Between 1850 and 1950 incomes increased eightfold, life expectancy rose twenty-eight years, and infant mortality fell from 15 to 2 percent. By 1950 Sweden was one of the richest countries in the world, and it still had a small government. Its total tax burden, at 19 percent of gross domestic product (GDP), was lower than that of the United States and other European countries.

It's only relatively recently that Sweden's tax burden and size of government have ballooned. Government spending exploded from 31 to 60 percent of GDP in the twenty years between 1960 and 1980. High taxes and big government spending alone don't constitute socialism, but they do have consequences. As Sweden's government grew, its economy stagnated. It was the fourth-richest country in the OECD (a group of rich countries) in 1970, but by 2000 it had fallen to fourteenth place. Sweden grew most when it was freer than it is today. But even today, it remains relatively economically free and prosperous, and its policies are far from socialist.

If Sweden isn't socialist, then what is? This is where Americans seem to be confused. Propagandists like Michael Moore don't help when they tweet out things like "Most polls now show young adults (18-35) across America prefer socialism (fairness) to capitalism (selfishness)." Socialism doesn't simply equal "fairness." What it really equals is the abolition of private property; in a socialist economy, the government decides what will be produced, how, and for whom.

Most countries are neither purely capitalist nor purely socialist. All capitalist economies allow, for good or ill, some government ownership of resources and centralized economic planning. Likewise, most socialist countries allow some degree of economic freedom—or they would suffer even worse economic consequences.

The Soviet Union during its period of War Communism (1918–21) and China during the Great Leap Forward (1958–62) came closest to abolishing private property. After each of these massive failures, the Communist governments offered limited private ownership of some means of production and allowed small markets to operate, though socialism predominated.

Today, there are only three countries that remain nearly entirely socialist: North Korea, Venezuela, and Cuba. Other officially socialist countries, like China, are only nominally so, but actually allow for so much private ownership and control that they qualify as mixed economies.

We'll visit these places and also three former Soviet countries that are trying to reform—Russia, Ukraine, and Georgia. We'll combine our firsthand travel observations with economic theory, history, and empirical social science to try and understand what's going on in these places.

For us, as travelers, socialist economic policies can be an inconvenience, but for those who live under them, they can impose brutal and unnecessary suffering, which makes us angry—and might make you angry too.

So, with that warning, pack your carry-on, order a stiff drink from the flight attendant, and let's embark on our tour of the unfree world.

CHAPTER ONE

STARVING SOCIALISM: VENEZUELA

JANUARY 2017

"**Y**ou guys need to go to Venezuela," our old friend, Marshall Stocker, told us over lobster and beer in New Hampshire in late July 2016. Marshall is a sort of "adventure capitalist." He was in Egypt doing real estate deals during the Arab Spring before he had to cut his losses and get out of town. Now he runs an emerging markets mutual fund for a big firm in Boston. Bob and I enjoy following his Facebook page, which highlights his travels to exotic locales like the jungles of Myanmar or the Mongolian desert as he looks for countries to invest in.

We agreed. Venezuela was on our list, but Venezuela is a complete fucking mess. Our wives, Lisa and Tracy, had already laid down the law—we weren't allowed to get killed or end up in prison while working on this book. I suppose bigger life insurance policies would've appeased them somewhat, but hey—neither of us has a death wish, either.

Marshall had a suggestion that made the trip sound safer and more practical. "Just fly into Colombia and travel to the Venezuelan border. You can check out what's going on from there and maybe venture across. That'll be safe enough. Besides, there's a lot of crazy economic activity on the border."

The more we thought about it, the better the idea sounded. Venezuela, the most recent darling of socialism's proponents, isn't tarnished with the same long history of political repression as other countries. Venezuela was an example of "democratic" socialism. At least until recently, it was the model that Western intellectuals admired and held up for emulation as a socialist paradise. Now things are falling apart, but the apologists still insist the country's problems have nothing to do with socialism.

Western intellectuals, whom Lenin called "useful idiots," tend to overlook or make excuses for socialist regimes' economic failures and humanitarian atrocities. Today, the idiots are running out of places to admire. Almost no sane person holds up North Korea as a model state.[1] While Castro apologists still tout Cuban health care and education, most everyone else recognizes that Cuba's Communist regime is politically repressive and economically backward.

Venezuela was supposed to be different. In 1992, Colonel Hugo Chávez was jailed for two years after a failed coup attempt. He then became a politician and won the 1998 presidential election with 56.2 percent of the vote, in what was viewed as a more or less fair election. Chávez established a new constitution in 1999 and was reelected a year later with 59.8 percent of the vote.

To many observers, Chávez's brand of "Bolívarian Socialism" (named after the nineteenth-century anti-colonialist revolutionary Simón Bolívar) seemed to be a success. In 2011, Bernie
Sanders claimed, "These days, the American dream is more apt
to be realized in South America, in places such as Ecuador,
Venezuela and Argentina, where incomes are actually more
equal today than they are in the land of Horatio Alger. Who's
the banana republic now?"[2]

Similarly, upon Chávez's death in 2013, the website Salon
published an article titled "Hugo Chávez's Economic Miracle"
which claimed that "Chávez racked up an economic record that
a legacy-obsessed American president could only dream of
achieving."[3]

We needed to experience this socialist paradise for ourselves.
After following the news stories about trade on the Colombia-
Venezuela border for a few months, we scheduled our trip. On
January 2, 2017, still sporting our respective New Year's hang-
overs, we took a short overnight flight from Dallas to Bogotá
and continued on to Cúcuta the next morning.

Cúcuta was a pleasant surprise. Colombia's sixth-largest
city, with a population of 650,000, Cúcuta boasted an impressive skyline, attractive architecture, and well-maintained office
buildings. The streets, though sometimes congested, were in
good condition. There were a variety of restaurants and shopping options within a short walk of our downtown hotel. When
we went out for drinks at night, we felt as safe as we would
anywhere else in Latin America.

We weren't there to see Cúcuta, though. We were there
because Cúcuta is on the west bank of the shallow and muddy
Río Táchira, where two bridges and other, unofficial river

crossings connect Colombia with Venezuela. This was where Venezuelans, in their early socialist days, had once smuggled goods into Colombia to be sold for market prices, and thus a profit. Today, it's where Venezuelans buy staple goods that are unavailable at home.

On our way to the Santander Bridge, which was the smaller of the two official crossings, we met up with Julian Villabona, a reporter with the PanAm Post. A mutual friend had introduced us to Julian, and he agreed to help us speak with people at the border while he wrote his own story for the Post's website.

After a short drive, the four-lane, paved road terminated at a dusty intersection near the Santander Bridge, which was closed to vehicular traffic. There were around a dozen small permanent roadside stores and at least twice as many temporary roadside stands, which offered a wide variety of basic goods and necessities—flour, cooking oil, sugar, toilet paper, candy, beans—as well as bigger-ticket items, like tires, that were in short supply in Venezuela.

The bridge swarmed with foot traffic. Every day, thousands of Venezuelans come with suitcases, bags, carts, backpacks, and crates, and load them with whatever they can afford and carry home. These weren't impoverished Venezuelans; these were members of the middle class who had the means to travel to the border and buy goods.

When we reached the Colombian checkpoint, halfway across the bridge, Julian asked what we wanted to do. The Colombian border police were checking passports only haphazardly; we could walk right into Venezuela if we wanted—but could we come back into Colombia?

Thousands crossed back and forth across this bridge between Venezuela and Colombia every day in search of basic necessities.

Julian had a brief conversation with the guard, who shrugged his shoulders, convincing Julian that reentry was *no hay problema* for two gringo economists and their guide, and we crossed into Venezuela. The Venezuelan checkpoint had a lone man in uniform. He didn't care about us either; he was too busy sorting through a woman's bags and confiscating items for himself.

Compared with the hustle and bustle of the shops on the Colombian side of the river, the Venezuelan side was eerily quiet. The official duty-free store had long since been abandoned. The only other establishment was a large gas station that had an attendant dutifully waiting at every pump.

The Venezuelan government subsidizes gasoline prices so that, at about fifty cents a gallon, Venezuela enjoys some of the world's cheapest gas. But even with fuel that cheap, there were no customers for the well-staffed gas station; Venezuela's socialist planners apparently hadn't foreseen that a bridge closed to vehicles might not have many customers.

As we walked toward the village of Ureña, Julian became visibly uncomfortable. Though we didn't have bags of goods to steal, Bob and I were the only Americans in sight, making us targets for robbery or kidnapping. We agreed it was best not to hang around too long in Venezuela, and technically, without visas, we were there illegally. We eventually switched directions, joined the Venezuelans heading west, and returned to Colombia without incident.

After perusing a few shops, we found what we required—Bahia, a Colombian *cerveza*. The shop fronted the dirt road and sported a few plastic chairs and a table. The music was loud, but the beer was cold and we had a good view of the comings and goings.

What we observed was a damned shame. Venezuela once boasted one of the freest economies in the world, according to Bob's index. In 1970, Venezuela scored 7.2, making it the world's tenth-freest economy. And when Venezuela's economy was free, the country was relatively prosperous. According to the World Bank, in 1967 the average Venezuelan was $1,995 richer than the average Spaniard.

But by 2014, the average Venezuelan earned only about $200 more than he had in 1967. In nearly fifty years, Venezuelans experienced essentially *zero* economic growth, while Spaniards had seen their average income more than double. And by some estimates, Venezuelan incomes have dropped 50 percent since 2014—so the economy has moved from stagnation to collapse. Today, Venezuela ranks dead last in the economic freedom index, with a score of about 3.[4]

As economists, Bob and I know that economic freedom almost inevitably leads to good economic outcomes, because free people have both the incentive and the ability to improve their own lives, and, in the process, the lives of others. Adam Smith put it best in his book *The Wealth of Nations* when he wrote of an "invisible hand" that guided individual economic self-interest to a greater good. As Smith put it: "Every individual ... neither intends to promote the public interest, nor knows how much he is promoting it ... he intends only his own security; and by directing that industry in such a manner as its produce may be of the greatest value, he intends only his own gain, and he is in this, as in many other cases, led by an invisible hand to promote an end which was no part of his intention."[5]

This "invisible hand" requires two things: freedom and the rule of law. Law is needed to secure property rights, and people need freedom to voluntarily trade goods and services at freely set prices.

Sitting in a market in Colombia, you can see in practice what economists can explain in theory. Free markets and market prices convey important information. They tell consumers whether a good is plentiful (and therefore cheap) or scarce (and therefore expensive). In turn, what consumers are willing to pay informs producers and entrepreneurs what goods are most valuable—something that can vary by time, place, and customer. The goal of the entrepreneur is to make money, not to promote economic efficiency or economic development. But by meeting customer demand, entrepreneurs inevitably make an economy more efficient and successful, *provided that the pricing system is accurate, which is what a free and open market ensures*. Anything that impedes free trade also impedes the accuracy of prices.

Even more fundamental is private property, which makes it possible to own, and therefore buy and sell, goods. Other factors are at play too, of course. Inflation, caused by the government's reckless printing of money, distorts prices. Taxes and regulations do the same by placing additional costs on trade.

When Venezuela was a freer economy, it was relatively prosperous. But as the government became more involved in regulating the economy, it became progressively less free, less efficient, and less productive. When Chávez came to power, this process was already well underway; he only doubled down on it and turned economic regression into economic disaster. Venezuela's insecure property rights, nationalized industries, punitive taxes, monetary inflation, and business-stifling regulations resulted in what we saw in vivid and heartbreaking detail at the Santander Bridge on the Colombian-Venezuelan border: impoverished middle-class Venezuelans, lugging home bundles of sugar, rice, beans, and diapers. We saw what economic theory can mean in economic fact.

Desperate Venezuelans line up trying to get an entry visa to Colombia. An estimated four million Venezuelans have fled the country since the crisis began.

The next morning, we went to the Simón Bolívar Bridge. Again, the Colombian side was alive with commerce, only more so: a chaotic jumble of people, delivery vehicles, buses, cabs, motorcycles, and push carts, maneuvering through a labyrinth of clogged, dusty roads lined with shops.

Vendors called out to Venezuelans coming into Colombia, and one woman's cry in particular—"¡*Compramos pelo*!"—caught our attention.

"Let's talk to her," I said. "I read about this."

Denise was known as a "dragger"—a middleman. She explained that she was finding Venezuelan women who wanted to sell their hair. She would bring them to a makeshift barbershop where their hair would be cut and used to make extensions.

"¿*Cuánto cuesta*?"

I wanted to know what she paid women for their hair. She shook her head, saying something I didn't understand. Julian explained, "She thinks you want to sell *your* hair. She doesn't want it. It's too short and red to be marketable."

Julian told her what I meant to say in Spanish, and she said the price varied depending on the quality and the length, but for very good, long hair, maybe as much as eighty U.S. dollars.

According to a Reuters article I'd read, mid-length hair fetched around sixty thousand Colombian pesos, which, at the time, was about twenty U.S. dollars. That might not sound like much, but it's about what a Venezuelan with a minimum wage job and food rations earns in a month. Here at the border, even twenty bucks would help bring home valuable necessities.

We ventured briefly into Venezuela again, but all the action was on the Colombian side of the border, so we came back and talked to Venezuelans lugging their heavy bags in the hot sun. Most seemed nervous and on guard—robberies are prevalent—and spoke only briefly and warily, telling us they came to buy necessities; they were generally more talkative entering Colombia than leaving it.

One obviously middle-class couple, Paulo and Ana María, talked at length with us. They had come from Ciudad Bolívar in far eastern Venezuela to buy supplies. According to Google Maps, Ciudad Bolívar is about 780 miles to the east, an estimated eighteen hours by car. The journey took them three days, they said, because it was too dangerous to drive at night.

Paulo told us, "We've come to buy rice, medicine, soap, shampoo, and other things, like car parts, unavailable at home." They had been coming to Colombia every three months, he added, but this was their last trip because "the danger from bandits is getting too great."

They had to make these journeys in the first place because of Venezuela's socialist policies, which had destroyed domestic production of basic goods and limited the availability of imports. In the early days of Chávez's presidency, annual food imports to Venezuela averaged about $75 per person. After Chávez confiscated more than ten million acres of private farmland, food production collapsed and food imports soared. By 2012, shortly before Chávez's death, food imports had reached an average of $370 per person each year. Today, the Venezuelan government can't afford to subsidize food imports, so the people have to find food on the black market—or in Colombia.

Julian told us about Sabrina Martin, a reporter working on a story about new bakery regulations in Venezuela. She told him that bakeries are supposed to buy imported flour from the government (which has a monopoly on imported flour). The government, however, does not have enough flour to meet demand;

government-imposed price controls make it impossible for the bakeries to turn a profit; and government regulations that require bakeries to offer bread throughout the business day mean that bakery owners have to break the law either by buying flour on the black market or by having bare shelves—and in either event they are expected to run their businesses at a loss.

We had read a similar story, in which the government confiscated millions of toys from a toy company and arrested its executives because the price of toys was allegedly too high! These stories are not uncommon in Venezuela. Sabrina interviewed Víctor Maldonado, executive director of the Chamber of Commerce, Industry, and Services of Caracas.[6] Maldonado reported that in 2016 alone, more than 30,000 Venezuelan companies closed. Venezuela had 800,000 companies before Hugo Chávez came to power in 1999, but only about 230,000 remain today.

The Confederation of Farmer Associations (Fedeagro) reported that the production of rice, corn, and coffee in Venezuela has fallen by 60 percent over the last decade. Similarly, the number of beef cattle in the country has decreased by 38 percent over the past five years according to Vicente Carrillo, the former president of Venezuela's cattle ranchers' association.

The collapse of private businesses has forced people to rely on the government for handouts, but there is never enough to go around. People line up early in the morning to get government-rationed food and supplies, but the lines are long, the items are few, and the recipients are targets for thieves.

That brings us back to the bridges near Cúcuta, where there are no government-monopoly wholesalers, no arbitrary price controls, no limits on profits, and where markets can provide what the Venezuelan government cannot.

The stores in Colombia were well stocked. There were three or four pharmacies near the bridge selling a wide variety of medicines and supplies. Bulk food was everywhere, and pallets of bags of rice were constantly being off-loaded from trucks and into the storefronts. Phone cards, cooking oil, diapers, pre-packaged snacks, juice drinks, and many other basic goods were widely available. There were roadside stands selling food and ice cream. According to Julian, prices were cheap, even by local standards. A pound of rice went for less than a dollar.

The only thing we couldn't find was beer. It was available for takeaway from stores, but we were looking for a place to sit and people-watch. Eventually we found a small, dusty place with a few beat-up plastic chairs that had a beer cooler. It wasn't on one of the main shopping alleys, but it was the only option around. We grabbed a couple Bahias, which cost about thirty-three cents each.

Not only were the beers cheap, but we counted ourselves fortunate because, to Venezuelans, beer had become something of a luxury. In Venezuela, six months earlier, there was no beer at all. That's right—*they ran out of beer*. Empresas Polar, the country's largest brewer, which produces 70 to 80 percent of Venezuela's beer, had closed all four of its breweries the previous April when they ran out of malted barley.

More accurately, the company ran out of foreign exchange necessary to buy imported barley.[7] Barley isn't grown in Venezuela's tropical climate. In a market economy, Empresas Polar would have traded domestic currency in the foreign exchange market to buy whatever imported ingredients it needed. But Venezuela's planners control access to foreign exchange and didn't allocate enough to the company to import the needed barley. Yet according to the government, the problem is that Lorenzo Mendoza, Polar's CEO, is a "thief and a traitor" trying to undermine the socialist regime.[8] Meanwhile, Venezuelans went thirsty.

As horrifying as a shortage of beer sounds, it's nowhere near the worst of Venezuela's problems. Venezuelans aren't just thirsty. They're hungry. Most Venezuelans don't have access to a market like the one we were at. As a result, according to a survey done by universities in Venezuela, three-quarters of adults had lost an average of nineteen pounds during 2016. Caritas, a Catholic humanitarian organization, found that among children under five years old, more than 11 percent suffered from moderate or severe malnutrition. The situation has only become worse since our visit. Venezuelans lost an average of twenty-four pounds in 2017.[9] Venezuela's socialist policies are literally starving the country.

Two months after our visit, the Ministry of Health released statistics showing that infant mortality rates had shot up 30 percent in 2016, and the minister who released the statistics was promptly fired. So much for Article 83 of Venezuela's constitution, which declares: "Health is a fundamental social right and the responsibility of the State, which shall guarantee it as part of the right to life." I guess no one told Chávez that writing down a "right" to something on a piece of paper doesn't magically make it materialize.

But it was certainly enough to fool the Hollywood Left. When Chávez died in 2013, Sean Penn wrote, "Today the people of the United States lost a friend it never knew it had. And poor people around the world lost a champion." Similarly, Oliver Stone, the chief idiot among the useful idiots, who produced a farce of a documentary on Chávez, *Mi Amigo Hugo*, that even *Foreign Policy* found "disgraceful," wrote, "I mourn a great hero to the majority of his people and those who struggle throughout the world for a place."[10] The ever-obnoxious Michael Moore tweeted, "Hugo

Chávez declared the oil belonged 2 the ppl. He used the oil $ 2 eliminate 75% of extreme poverty, provide free health & education 4 all. That made him dangerous."

No, what made him dangerous—to the Venezuelan people— was that high oil prices disguised how he was destroying the country's economy. After Venezuela became an unmistakable economic basket case, the Hollywood sycophants and lefties like Bernie Sanders suddenly went quiet. But when pressed, the useful idiots blamed Venezuela's collapse on falling oil prices, as if it were a natural calamity that could afflict any country.

But the truth is, not only had prices fallen, *so had Venezuela's oil production.* Despite sitting on the world's largest known oil reserves, oil production was at a twenty-three-year low, *because of socialism.* Nationalized oil companies hadn't maintained their pipelines and refineries, because they had no profit motive to do so.

Kevin Grier, an economist colleague of mine at Texas Tech, co-authored a cool, empirical study that compared the performance of Venezuela's economy during the oil boom against the economies of similar, but non-socialist, countries. Guess what? Venezuela's economy had improved, but by less than that of the other countries; in fact, Kevin says that if Venezuela had not followed socialist policies, Venezuelan incomes would have been 20 to 30 percent higher. What high oil prices had done was hide that Venezuela was falling behind its neighbors economically and just keeping pace when it came to measurements of poverty and infant mortality. Once oil prices fell, the mask was off.

So with production cratering and oil revenues drying up, where is the Venezuelan government getting its money? That's easy. They're running a printing press, and you don't have to be a drunk economist to know that results in inflation. Prices are rising faster and faster every year—from over 30 percent in 2008 to as high as 1,600 percent in 2016, according to media reports. Today it is even worse. Inflation was estimated at 18,000 percent in March and April 2018 alone.[11] The reality is it's almost impossible to measure inflation properly in a country with such massive shortages and controlled prices.

Hyperinflation is one of the most destructive things a government can do to an economy. It devastates the balance sheets of banks and other lenders, and as a result, borrowing and lending grind to a halt. Virtually every house, factory, and business you've ever seen was created with borrowed funds, and failing banks mean no new houses, factories, or businesses. Inflation destroys savings and people's ability to make long-term plans and turns the entire economy into an attempt to spend money as fast as possible before it loses its value.

With our last cold(ish) beer behind us, we ventured back into the melee of shoppers and asked Julian if we could trade for some Venezuelan currency. We had only a few Colombian pesos and he wasn't sure if they'd take dollars. There were official-looking dealers in kiosks and dozens of unofficial dealers roaming the streets.

Bob walked up to one fellow with a twenty-dollar bill in hand and mimed that he'd like to change it for *bolívares*. The guy handed over a twelve-inch stack of hundred-bolívar notes, which was the highest denomination in circulation at the time. Bob asked if he had any smaller notes, and he laughed, dug around in his bag, and threw in a couple bundles of twenties and fifties. "¡*Gratis*!" he laughed.

You'd need at least a five-foot stack of *bolívares* to buy something worth a hundred dollars. Julian told us that they don't even count the bills for large transactions. They just weigh them. In fact, we had noticed that some of the Venezuelans appeared to have heavy luggage coming *into* Colombia. It suddenly dawned on us that the incoming bags were filled with cash.

We thought about taking the nearly worthless stack of notes to a strip club in Cúcuta to "make it rain," but decided that pissing off Colombian strippers was not very prudent. In the end, we opted to do our small bit to fight Venezuelan inflation by taking the money out of circulation and bringing the stack of bills home as souvenirs.

As we walked toward the queue of yellow taxis waiting to take the richer Venezuelans, and us, to Cúcuta, Bob asked a passerby, "*¿Por qué vienes aquí?*" Why are you coming here?

He looked across the bridge he'd just crossed and muttered simply, "*No hay nada allí.*" There is nothing there.

For much of 2017, Chávez's successor, President Nicolás Maduro, had an approval rating that hovered between 20 and 30 percent, and anti-government protests abounded. But Maduro was reelected in 2018 amid, as the *New York Times* put it, "widespread disillusionment," with "more than half of voters not casting ballots," and critics alleging that the election was "heavily rigged."[12]

This shouldn't surprise anyone, because political freedom cannot survive without a large degree of economic freedom. In his 1944 book, *The Road to Serfdom*, Friedrich Hayek argued that a competitive capitalist economy is necessary to sustain democracy, and that once a country becomes "dominated by a collectivist creed, democracy will inevitably destroy itself."[13]

Similarly, in 1962, Milton Friedman noted: "Historical evidence speaks with a single voice on the relation between political freedom and a free market. I know of no example in time or place of a society that has been marked by a large measure of political freedom, and that has not also used something comparable to a free market to organize the bulk of economic activity."[14]

The reason is simple. Centrally planned, socialist economic systems necessarily concentrate economic power in the hands of government planners who can, through their economic edicts, punish dissent. This is exactly what has happened in Venezuela, where state employees were fired for signing a petition demanding a recall election of Maduro. In 2017 President Maduro ordered a special election for a Constituent Assembly that could rewrite the constitution and give him even greater power. While the opposition called for an electoral boycott, the government again threatened state employees to support Maduro or be fired. According to Reuters, the vice president of the state-owned oil company, Petroleos de Venezuela SA, told his employees "Any manager, superintendent, and supervisor who tries to block the Constituent Assembly, who does not vote, or whose staff does not vote, must leave his job on Monday."[15]

During the 2018 presidential election, the government banned the largest opposition parties, violently repressed anti-government protests, and moved the election forward seven months to hamper challengers. Many voters went directly from the voting booth to nearby "Red Spots," where the government checked their IDs and handed out food rations—essentially a bribe for voting.

Finally in 2019, a constitutional crisis erupted as Juan Guiadó was declared interim-president by the opposition-controlled National Assembly. He was quickly recognized by the United States and most nations in the Western Hemisphere and Europe as the legitimate leader of the country. As I write this, the Venezuelan military as well as the usual suspects (Cuba, North Korea, Nicaragua, etc.) are standing by Maduro. Guiadó's party, while less extreme than Maduro's, is a member of the Socialist International, so we have our doubts about whether this change will really matter.

Venezuela began its experiment with democratic socialism twenty years ago. Despite its democratic origins and a stroke of good fortune with an oil boom, socialism failed in Venezuela as it has failed everywhere else, bringing economic misery and political tyranny in its wake.

CHAPTER TWO

SUBSISTENCE SOCIALISM: CUBA

MAY 2016

E ven during the period when President Obama relaxed travel rules, Americans had a hard time getting to Cuba. Under our laws, it is illegal for American tourists to visit the island; as professors, though, Bob and I are allowed to go for research purposes.

There were no commercial flights from the United States to Cuba when we traveled there in 2016, but you could get there on a charter flight.[1] We booked two seats for the forty-one-minute flight from Miami to Havana for a whopping $459 each. Our commercial flights from Texas to Miami cost another couple hundred bucks apiece. A $700 fare should land you in London or Paris; instead we landed in Havana.

When we stepped off the charter plane onto the tarmac at 8:30 a.m., it felt like any place in the Caribbean—warm and humid, but not unpleasant. In fact, nothing was unpleasant at first. We proceeded through customs with minimal hassle and exchanged a thousand U.S. dollars into convertible pesos. Usually, neither of us would exchange that much at the airport, because airports offer some of the worst exchange rates you'll find while traveling. Cuba is different. The government owns all the banks, hotels, and exchange counters and offers the same rate everywhere. You can't find a better deal, so there's no point trying.

Independent of its economic system, almost every country has a few nice hotels and restaurants. In government-directed economies, a disproportionate amount of money is spent on what political leaders desire—typically, great Olympic sports teams, and a few showcase hotels and restaurants to impress foreigners. In Cuba's case, this included the opulent Hotel Nacional, reportedly one of the world's great hotels. But we were on a mission to see what life was like inside Cuba's socialist system. We couldn't experience that by drinking Cuba libres at a fancy resort, but we weren't going to sandbag it either. Neither of us is into unnecessary suffering.

Our first night was at a supposed three-star hotel on the coast in the Western suburbs of Havana, recommended by Bob's Mexican friend José Torra. Our reservation included a shuttle from the airport, but the driver never showed up. Cabs were plentiful, so it wasn't a big deal. We jumped into a modern, yellow, Chinese-made car with air-conditioning and paid a twenty-five-dollar fare. We didn't know it at the time, but it was the nicest car we would get into until our wives picked us up from our respective airports a week later.

The Hotel Neptuno Tritón opened in 1979, during the heyday of Cuban-Soviet cooperation. It has two towers, each looking like a Soviet housing project, protruding some twenty stories into the sky. The towers were once gleaming white, if the poster in the hotel lobby can be believed, but thirty-seven years of diesel fuel emissions and neglect have turned them a sickly tan color. Most of the windows on the upper floors were broken.

The lobby, though not air-conditioned, was well maintained. Bob had reserved two rooms for thirty-three bucks apiece with his credit card through a British website. Thanks to the American government's rules against American companies doing business with Cuba, American credit cards don't work anywhere on the island. Booking with a British middleman is a workaround. Bob strode up to the registration desk and said, "*Tenemos una reservacion.*"

Bob's Spanish is better than mine, which is to say he can *habla poco*. I picked up what little Spanish I know through traveling in Spanish-speaking countries and playing basketball with Puerto Ricans. That means I can order in restaurants and bars, demand a basketball, and express my displeasure when I don't get it. Bob did most of the talking on this trip.

The desk clerk typed frantically on her computer while engaging Bob in an equally frantic conversation in Spanglish.

He told me, "They can't find our reservation. She'll contact the British company and recommends we wait in the lobby." We opted to wait in the bar instead.

Cristal is Cuba's lighter beer, at 4.9 percent alcohol. The other beer, Bucanero, is slightly stronger at 5.5 percent and has a bit more flavor. That's the extent of the beer variety in Cuba. But hey, it's better than Venezuela. At least Cuba hadn't run out of beer, though beer shortages have occurred here as well.[2]

Two Cristals later, the desk clerk motioned Bob back to the counter. She could not reach the British company. Bob solved the problem the capitalist way. He paid sixty dollars cash for one room with two beds.

Two *cervezas* didn't give me beer goggles strong enough to overlook the shoddiness of the hotel. Three out of the four elevators were out of service, and we waited what seemed like forever before we decided to hoof it up the five flights of stairs with our bags. We found our room down the dark hallway, and Bob needed both the key and his shoulder to open the door.

At first the room seemed okay. The beds were neatly made, and despite missing a knob, the air conditioner turned on and blew cold air. That was important, since I was sweating like a whore in church after climbing all those stairs.

From the balcony, with its cracked glass railing, we had a view of the ocean, the deteriorating twin tower, and an abandoned court-yard. The bathroom, however, was the real gem. One of the metal ceiling panels was missing; there was mold everywhere; and, as we'd find out the next morning, running water was not guaranteed.

Bob and I have hiked many mountains together, and we've spent plenty of nights sleeping on the ground. We've definitely gone without indoor plumbing. This was nothing we couldn't handle. We decided to go relax at the pool.

Luckily, we caught the elevator as it rumbled to a stop at our floor. It was stuffed with people and their belongings, and as we squeezed in, I had some idea of what it would feel like to leave Cuba by boat.

The pool wasn't any better. Empty beer cans floated in the cloudy water. The twenty seats of the swim-up bar had long since deteriorated, and the mirror behind the bar was broken. Luckily there was a snack bar that sold beer. Our immediate surroundings at the decaying hotel were mostly offset by the nice ocean view, as long as you ignored the litter-strewn beach and the abandoned oil tank half-submerged in the rocky sand.

Before the revolution, Cuba had a thriving urban middle class, along with widespread rural poverty. Twentieth-century socialists claimed socialism would deliver greater equality and out-produce capitalism by ending wasteful competition, business cycles, and predatory monopolies. Socialism hasn't delivered the goods it promised in Cuba or anywhere else. Today, Cuba is a poor country made poorer by socialism.

Here's why: almost a hundred years ago, the Austrian economist Ludwig von Mises explained that socialism, even if run by benevolent despots and populated with workers willing to work for the common good, could still not match capitalism's performance. Socialism requires abolishing private property in the means of production. But private property is necessary to have the free exchange of labor, capital, and goods that establish proper prices. Without proper prices, socialist planners could not know which consumer goods were needed or how best to produce them. Socialist planners often compensate for their lack of market pricing by relying on prices from foreign capitalist countries or their own country's black-market prices, but foreign-market prices and internal black-market prices are obviously poor equivalents to local free-market—another way of saying "accurate"—prices.

Socialism also gives tremendous power to government officials and bureaucrats who are the system's planners—and with that power comes corruption, abuse, and tyranny. It is no accident that the worst democides of the twentieth century occurred in socialist countries like the Soviet Union, Communist China, and Nazi (National Socialist) Germany, where planners simply decided to eliminate populations they thought interfered with their plans.[3]

The democides were justified in the name of making a "new socialist man," a perfect worker who would outperform his exploited capitalist counterpart, but that guy never showed up. Socialist workers chronically *underperform* because they and their managers are not rewarded for their performance. Workers and managers in a capitalist system are rewarded, and so have an incentive to do better, to innovate, to experiment, and to gain new knowledge and skills.

The Hotel Tritón's decaying edifice was a crumbling tribute to Cuba's central-planning problems. Cuba had the resources to make large capital investments in state-run enterprises when it received aid from the Soviet Union. But many of these hotels can't generate enough revenue to sustain the initial investment. Cuban government planners then had to pick which hotels to subsidize to prevent decay. The Hotel Tritón didn't make the cut. It was rotting, inside and out. And nobody cared because nobody owned it.

After about half an hour of sitting by the pool I'd had enough relaxation. "This place sucks."

"Socialism sucks," said Bob as he drained his beer. "Let's go into the city and see what's happening."

After a thirty-minute ride in a Soviet-made Lada, which is best described as a life-sized Matchbox car without the bells or whistles, our driver dropped us off in La Habana Vieja, or Old Havana. Most tourists visit this district to see the old churches and the historic fort, but we were there to check out the commerce. We discovered that fifty-eight years of socialism had not succeeded in stamping out the entrepreneurial spirit of the Cuban people.

"Señor, you want cigars? It is a special day. Fifty percent off Cohibas. Come with me."

We heard about ten different versions of the same pitch dozens of times during our trip. It seemed every day was a "special day," and nearly every Cuban in the streets had a place where we could get "authentic" Cuban cigars at a substantial discount. Government-operated stores and factories monopolize the Cohibas and other name brands and sell them at prices few Cubans can afford, so Cubans smoke cheaper cigars, and the street hawkers scam tourists into buying them, repackaged with name-brand labels and souvenir-worthy boxes. It seems like a steal. And it is—for the sellers.

To be fair, not all the street entrepreneurs were frauds. Plenty of Cubans huddled in stairways and other alcoves, where they displayed paintings or other handicrafts for sale. But none of these goods were sold from permanent commercial establishments.

After ten minutes of walking Bob quietly observed, "There aren't any stores. No advertisements." It wasn't entirely true. There were a few stores, but the paucity of normal commerce was striking.

In a capitalist economy, entrepreneurs create businesses to make profits, which they earn by pleasing their customers. But in a socialist system, a bureaucrat decides which businesses can open, where they can operate, and what they can sell, and he really doesn't care what the customer thinks. Adopting a socialist system is like turning your whole economy into a giant Department of Motor Vehicles.

Our strategy for seeing Havana was simple: walk until we got too hot, stop for beers until we felt refreshed, and repeat as necessary. The absence of commercial signs made this harder than one would think. Restaurants and bars were easy enough to identify once we were standing in front of them. But it was hard to stand on any street corner and distinguish residential streets from commercial streets. This is not a symptom of poverty. Go to any non-socialist poor country in the world and there is no shortage of advertisements and signs. Beer companies subsidize the signs of retailers serving their products in almost every country on the globe. But not in Cuba. The problem is that no one makes any more or less money whether you find your way into their store or not. So nobody gives enough of a damn to put up a sign.

At one beer stop in Central Havana, well away from the tourist area of Habana Vieja, we found ourselves in the midst of a happy-hour crowd. There were many attractive young women. The music was loud and very good, and the alcohol was flowing.

For the record, Bob and I both married our high school sweethearts, and while we may drink a lot while traveling, we are not looking for sex. The risks of disease and divorce are too high a price to pay for a quick lay. (And because we know our wives will read this, it is also very, very wrong.)

One young *chica* struck up a conversation in Spanish with Bob and invited us to hang out with her and her friends. We knew the drill by that point. At best, they were looking for some rich tourists to buy them food and drinks all night. At worst, we would end up bruised and naked on the outskirts of Havana. Bob declined repeatedly until she went away. As we left, a different *chica* followed us out to repeat the same offer but with something obviously more explicit in mind.

In Central Havana, the lack of commerce unrelated to tobacco, alcohol, or sex was striking. *Habaneros* lived in these neighborhoods. So where did they shop?

We found one store that was a large open room with high ceilings and cement support columns. The space could have easily housed a factory. Instead, on the right side of the room was a long orange lunch counter with fried chicken, rice, and fried plantains on the menu. On the left side of the room, behind a counter, there were shelves with bottles of rum, cases of the local cola, a few canned goods, cartons of eggs, and large sacks of rice next to a scale. A line of Cubans shopped their way down the counter. The place was an odd mix, somewhere between the worst imaginable version of a grade school cafeteria and a grocery in which 95 percent of the stock is depleted.

The limited number of product choices and the eclectic, even illogical, product mix is typical of Cuban stores. A small store on a main avenue in Central Havana sold plumbing fittings, dresses, candles, and some sort of cleaning material. We did find a convenience-style store with what you might expect: soda, juice, bottled water, snack food, cigarettes, and some canned goods. But in this store, and every other store, in each product category you had one choice, whether it was one type of detergent, one type of paper towel, or one brand of flour. Bob tried to take a picture, but a clerk told him that photos weren't allowed in stores.

Cuba's socialist economy manages to produce some items, but notice the utter lack of variety.

Almost by accident, we found an indoor shopping mall. We saw no signs, but happened by when someone opened the door, treating us to a refreshing blast of air conditioning. The selection of products here was somewhat better, but still very limited. Bob summed up the Havana shopping scene in four words: "This is just sad." I tried to find a Coke, but of course that was nearly impossible. All they had was their one brand of what I called "Commie Cola."

Still, not everything in Cuba is completely state-run. In 1997, it became legal for Cubans to register a business and rent out up to two rooms in their private residences. More recently, the two-room restriction was lifted and homeowners were allowed to hire non-family members to work for them, and the state's per-room tax was lowered 25 percent. Since then, the rental housing market has flourished.

To investigate the contrast between the state-run hotels and the privately owned *casas particulares*, I booked two nights in a *casa* in Central Havana. The owner was married to an Irishman and lived most of the year in Ireland, but a neighbor named Laura met us outside the three-story apartment building. The exterior was unremarkable—white with green paint and balconies on most units, with clotheslines hanging from them.

Laura greeted us promptly and, unlike Hotel Tritón, had record of our payment through Airbnb. At the top of two flights of stairs, she opened the door to a well-kept, two-bedroom apartment. There was a combined living room and kitchenette, a room with a double bed, and one with two singles. The bathroom was clean, stocked with toilet paper, and had reliable hot water. The two air-conditioning units worked well, and the balcony had a view of the ocean and the Malecón, Havana's famous seafront promenade. Bob wasn't sure what Malecón meant, but he joked that it could be translated as "bad econ," and that sounded about right. At fifty-seven dollars a night the apartment was three bucks cheaper than Hotel Tritón but vastly nicer, and in a much better location.

The stark difference between the government-run hotel and the private apartment rental was not a fluke. After spending two nights in our Central Havana *casa particular,* we took a grueling six-hour drive to the old Spanish colonial town of Trinidad on the south-central coast. Trinidad, founded in 1514, was a major center for the sugar and slave trades, and in 1988, it was named a UNESCO World Heritage Site. We arrived without lodging reservations because we had read in the guidebook that there were more than five hundred private apartments and rooms available for rent in the small town.

Our enterprising driver tried to direct us to the *casa particular* of a friend, but we declined. We felt we'd overpaid for the lunch he had arranged on the drive over, and insisted on going to Plaza Mayor, the central town square. After six sweaty, windblown hours in a '51 Plymouth, we didn't care where we'd sleep that night. All we wanted was cold beer, and lots of it.

We walked about twenty paces and came upon a decent-looking bar with fans, and we were on our second beer when we noticed that the guy at the next table was using an old 1950s Russian-made, cabinet-style TV as a chair, while two chairs hung upside-down nearby on the wall as decorations. That image captured perfectly the relative price structure in Cuba.

Our server noticed our bags and asked if we needed a room. At first I refused, because we had heard room rates go up five dollars when a middleman brings you to the house. But she said that the owner had an apartment available above the bar. Not lugging a bag in the heat sounded appealing. So did having a fully stocked bar right downstairs! I left Bob with the bags and headed upstairs to meet the owner. Bob warned me that fifty U.S. dollars was the max he was willing to pay.

The room was large, clean, and well-kept, with two single beds, cold AC, and a bathroom with reliable hot and cold water. There was a large patio with tables, chairs, and ashtrays that would be great for me to continue chain-smoking cigars after Bob crashed for the night.

"*¿Le cuenta noche?*" I asked my host, glad that Bob wasn't there to make fun of my awful Spanish.

"*Veinticinco.*" Twenty-five dollars. We took it for two nights.

We returned to Central Havana two days later, again without a reservation. We'd planned to continue staying at *casas particulares* since the other two had been so nice. But we were again hot, battered, and grumpy after the long drive, so the first priorities were beer and food, in that order. About a ten-minute walk from the Capitol, we found a place for lunch with a balcony and a breeze on one of the old main boulevards that had a wide, tree-lined walking path in its center. The government-owned Hotel Caribbean was two doors down.

I asked Bob to check it out because I was tired of lugging my bag around in the heat. Bob had the hotel staff show him the room before he booked, and I can only assume the ice-cold AC desensitized him to the filth that surrounded him, because he reserved it for fifty dollars for the night.

Yes, the AC was refreshing, but the broken bathroom door, cracked toilet seat, shower mold, lack of any hot water, leftover soap used by the previous guest, hole in my towel, suspicious-looking stain on Bob's towel, and used drinking glass that came out of a bag labeled "sanitized" were considerably less impressive.

The state-owned hotels in Cuba suck, but they don't suck because Cuba is poor. They suck because no one cares. The people who own *casas particulares* care because they profit when people opt to stay in them. Their desire for more money leads them to reinvest some of their revenue to maintain and improve their property, so that more people will choose to stay with them in the future.

Private property rights give people the incentive to preserve resources (like housing) for the future. The managers of the state-owned hotels don't have the same incentive because they don't benefit from the hotel being in better condition in the future.

What is true for accommodation is also true for food, as we discovered throughout our trip. On our second morning in Havana, after we had left the Hotel Tritón, we asked a taxi driver to drop us at a restaurant near our *casa particular*. He dropped us off in front of a nondescript, multistory building. There was a large open door and a well-maintained staircase but otherwise nothing to distinguish this building from any other. Once we climbed the stairs, things were entirely different.

El Guajirito is one of approximately two thousand private restaurants in Havana. Cuba began allowing private restaurants in 1993, but at that time they were limited to no more than twelve seats, prohibited from serving seafood and beef, and required to pay very high taxes. By 2010, the official state media reported that no more than seventy-four private restaurants were operating in all of Havana. In 2011, the restrictions were relaxed; restaurants could now seat up to fifty people. Prohibitions on serving beef and seafood were also lifted.

El Guajirito had three large, air-conditioned dining areas and a well-stocked bar. The whole place was decorated in a sort of Latin American cowboy theme. The large, commercial-grade, stainless steel kitchen could have been in any high-end restaurant in the United States.

Bob was as eager to eat there as I was. "This place would pass any health inspection in the States." The amount of capital invested was impressive indeed.

"The local talent is nice, too." Bob pointed out an attractive young waitress wearing a short skirt, sexy cowboy-style blouse, and a cowboy hat. Everyone on the waitstaff was attractive, and they all spoke English as well as anyone we met in Cuba. In short, the human capital matched the physical capital that was invested in the place.

We started with a house cocktail, which was more "girly" than we expected, and then ordered a bottle of wine and an appetizer. My meal of shrimp, Caribbean lobster tail, and fish was quite good, as was Bob's *ropa vieja*.

Over a dessert mojito we asked the general manager about the laws governing the size of private restaurants, because this place clearly seated more than fifty people.

"American spies! Trying to figure out our system!" he joked. Funny, but he was avoiding the question, so we asked again. He eventually shrugged, put his hand over his eyes, and said, "Well, I don't know. There may be a little..." and his voice wandered off. As far as we could gather, that meant the restaurant could be large—unofficially, of course—if you knew how to work the system. We'd later learn that some restaurants obtain separate licenses for a café and a restaurant and then combine them in order to get around the fifty-person limit.

We ate at private restaurants for most of the week. None of the others was as fancy as El Guajirito, but most served equally good meals. And that was the problem. The menus were virtually identical everywhere. Socialism claims to promote equality, but frequently what it delivers is just sameness.

There's only so much private enterprise restaurants can do to improve Cuba's gastronomically challenged culinary scene, because they all face the same difficulty getting ingredients from the country's state-controlled food industry. Over the course of the week, we came to realize that the same couple dozen items were on every menu, usually similarly prepared. The lack of spices and seasonings was noticeable. Some restaurants have "mules" who smuggle ingredients back from the United States, Spain, and Mexico. Tabasco is a popular item for them to transport, and Bob used it at almost every meal.

After a week with no variety in our diets, we decided on our last evening on the island to try a state-owned "Italian" restaurant on the main boulevard between the shitty Hotel Caribbean and the Capitol. We were disappointed to see that Italian meant nothing more than a few basic pizzas and a couple types of pasta, along with the same chicken, pork, seafood, and beef dishes we found everywhere else.

We ordered two beers and "mozzarella from the oven" as an appetizer. To say that it was the equivalent of Taco Bell queso with tomato chunks in it would be insulting to Taco Bell. In fact, it was a steaming pot of greasy white goo. We left without ordering more and found a private rooftop restaurant across the street. The menu had the usual stuff, but we picked it because of its location.

In most of the world, there are trade-offs between price, quality, and location. In Cuban restaurants, whether state-owned or private, prices for a meal ranged between fifteen and eighteen dollars, and the quality and variety were about the same across most establishments. In America, price influences your decision. Steak versus hamburger? A nice restaurant with fancy service or a casual place? Mixed drinks or beer? In Cuba, the prices are the same everywhere, so we ate a lot of lobster, sat in nicer outdoor venues, and drank more rum than beer.

I'm sure it's tempting to read "lobster, outdoor balconies, rum" and think, "That doesn't sound too bad." And for you, it might not be. But most Cubans can't afford to eat at the places we ate, and Cuba's socialist economic system can't even deliver variety to rich tourists. We were tired of the food after a week. But we could leave; Cubans are stuck with lousy food (outside the private restaurants), limited ingredients, and little variety for as long as they're stuck with socialism.

The lack of competition and free-market pricing in Cuba's economy leads to other social consequences as well. Bob's colleague at Southern Methodist University, W. Michael Cox, says that the reason Cuba generates so many great musicians is that they basically get paid the same as everyone else—so why do a dirty job like plumbing, when you can sing and play in a bar? As with the lobster, outdoor balconies, and rum, this might sound good at first. But when you pay people the same for pleasant jobs as you do for dirty jobs you get left with clogged pipes and the lack of reliable running water we experienced in Hotel Tritón.

Nowhere was Cuba's confused price structure more evident than in the automobile market. Traveling around the country, we saw a lot of cool cars, and even though it's a cliché to write about them, we have to admit it was pretty cool riding around Havana in 1950s American cars. Why are the cars so old? Because the government controls the supply of cars through import restrictions, and people can't afford them.

There's no reliable way to calculate Cuba's per capita income. The World Bank doesn't even attempt to count the number of Cuban people living in extreme poverty, and Bob's economic freedom index doesn't include Cuba because he can't get enough reliable data to rank it (though we're pretty sure it belongs at the bottom with Venezuela). It's more straightforward when you calculate the gross domestic product (GDP) per person in a market economy. GDP is just a measure of the dollar value of all the new goods and services sold during a year. In market economies, where prices are formed on the basis of supply and demand, we can add up all of the transactions to arrive at a rough approximation of the value created in that economy. In Cuba, the government is responsible for many of the purchases and it controls the prices. It's nearly meaningless to add up all the transactions, because the prices don't reflect the value to consumers.

About 70 percent of Cubans work for the state at an average salary of only twenty-five dollars per month. Of course, that doesn't count the zero-cost social services and subsidized housing and utilities, so in reality Cubans are richer than that. Still, while estimates may vary, the bottom line is this: Cubans are poor.

The Cuban government banned the importation of cars for more than fifty years. Until recently, only people with special "letters of authorization" from the Ministry of Transportation could bring in cars. In December 2013, the Cuban government decided to gradually import automobiles again, but prices remained high.

According to Cubans we asked, 1950s American cars—maintained merely to the point where they can function—sell for around $15,000, probably triple what they would cost in the United States in their condition. Amazingly, even the disgusting old Russian

Ladas and Moskvitches sell for $8,000 to $10,000. It turns out the supply and demand lessons we've taught our students all these years are correct. Despite the low incomes and thus low demand for cars, if supply is restricted enough, prices will skyrocket.

We thought the old cars were quaint and cool when we were driven short distances around Havana. But an eight-hour road trip in a '58 Mercury was a different story. When the highway was in decent shape and the morning air circulated freely through the large windows we were okay, but when the road deteriorated, our speed slowed, the air grew hotter, and the old car's weak suspension bounced along, we became two hot and cranky Americans, no longer entertained by the regime's multiple "bridges to nowhere" that spanned the highway or by our driver's $150 fare (six times the average monthly wage).

By the time we reached the small village of Puerto Esperanza on the north coast, I had sweated enough to get a serious case of swamp ass. Luckily there was a local's bar on the seaside and a couple beers reinforced our will to continue on.

Bob and Ben take a beer break from their steamy ride in the Cuban countryside. The old American cars aren't so cool on a six-hour drive. Import restrictions also make them ludicrously expensive.

We resumed our journey eastward. That is, until the road abruptly ended in a three-foot drop! The Mercury's drum brakes narrowly stopped us from plunging over the edge. The map had given us no warning of the dead end, and it was a long road back.

The next day, it was more of the same on a hot, uncomfortable, six-hour journey to Trinidad. This time we engaged a driver with a blue '51 Plymouth for a whopping $200 fare. We'd paid through the nose for two days of hot and miserable travel, so we decided to treat ourselves to an air-conditioned bus ride back to Havana, at the bargain price of $25. We went to the bus station, but before we could buy our tickets, we were lured away with the promise of an air-conditioned car, shared with two other people for the same price as the bus. The car would be much faster, we were told.

Turns out that assurance was too good to be true. The AC wasn't working in the 1991 Peugeot that came for us the next morning. The other two passengers didn't show up, so we waited while the driver hustled to find someone to add to our car. The suspension on the 1991 was a big improvement from the '58 Mercury, though, and we shaved about an hour off the drive time. But the heat and windburn still sucked.

Cubans pay dearly for slight improvements in car quality. In any rich country in the world, that Peugeot would be a $500 beater, at best a high school kid's first car. Bob said, "Man, if you found this car on a south Dallas used car lot, the dealer would give it to you for the cost of registration and title." Yet the people we talked to told us a Peugeot like that could sell for more than $30,000! Yes, you read that right. Relative to income this would be the equivalent of $280,000 in the United States. It's no wonder that in most areas we visited outside of Havana, Cubans get around on horseback or in horse-drawn wagons.

Reflecting on the car prices in Cuba left us mildly discouraged at the prospects for market reforms. Make no mistake, reforms are coming to Cuba, just as they came to China and will eventually come to Venezuela and North Korea. But reform is hard.

One of the problems of reforming a socialist economy is what economist Gordon Tullock called "the transitional gains trap," which means that while market reforms benefit everyone in the long run, in the short run, some people, who aren't even prospering at present, will lose valuable assets tied to the current socialist system. For instance, someone paid $30,000 for that '91 Peugeot. Their high fares aren't making them well-off because of their high up-front cost of the car. That car, one of the most valuable assets any Cuban can possibly own, will become nearly worthless once Cuba allows wide access to new, imported cars. If you're one of the thousands of current Cuban car owners, you won't want that to happen.

New cars aren't the only thing that's missing in Cuba. "Where are all the boats?" Bob wondered. He paused a moment, and then joked, "I guess they're all in Miami." Once you notice it, it's hard to notice anything else. The Havana harbor and other coastal areas we visited were devoid of boats. No sailboats, no Jet Skis, no ferries, *nada*. You had to wonder how they got their seafood. On one occasion, we did see a handful of small fishing boats moored at Puerto Esperanza, but otherwise it was just plain weird. No country is too poor to afford sailboats, but Havana's harbor was empty.

Just as we saw no boats, outside the airport we saw no airplanes, either. At night, Havana, a city of two million people, is eerily quiet; you rarely hear any traffic.

That quiet helps to explain a Cuban anomaly. Cuban health statistics are remarkably good for a country that is so poor. Usually, wealth and health go together. Most left-leaning people in the

United States will attribute Cuba's remarkable health statistics to its socialized medicine. The second hit (right behind Wikipedia) on a Google search for "Cuba's health care" is a *HuffPost* article titled "Cuba's Health Care System: A Model for the World." The World Health Organization director-general, Margaret Chan, is quoted in the article praising Cuba's leadership for "having made health an essential pillar of development."[4]

Official Cuban health statistics are impressive. Life expectancy in Cuba is 79.5 years, and the infant mortality rate is 4.4 deaths per 1,000 live births. Both of those figures are better than the same figures for the United States. Yet, we also know that the hospitals most Cubans use are so poorly equipped that people often have to bring their own sheets. What gives? The silence is part of the answer.

The lack of automobiles also means a lack of traffic fatalities. Since automobile accidents are a leading cause of death among younger people, the lack of automobiles has a disproportionate impact on life expectancy statistics for reasons that have nothing to do with health care.

The low rate of infant mortality is a product of data manipulation. At seventy-two abortions per one hundred births, Cuba has one of the highest abortion rates in the world, and Cuban doctors routinely force women to abort high-risk pregnancies so that Cuba's bureaucrats can brag about their health statistics. If you correct the data to account for these factors, Cuba's health statistics look a lot less impressive.[5]

One quiet evening, we walked up to the Malecón for drinks. The Malecón is the seawall along the bay where people go to stroll in the evenings. The sky turns romantically red at sunset, which makes it particularly popular with young couples. This is world-class real estate. In the mile or so stretch we walked, there were about three government-run restaurants. That's it. Three. We walked past decrepit buildings that looked empty, but were probably still serving as housing, and multiple empty lots going to seed. Can you imagine decaying buildings and empty lots for miles on end in any seaside city in the world? It just doesn't make sense, at least in a world with a working price system where highly valued real estate attracts investment.

Bob decided we needed to see the University of Havana and then the Plaza de la Revolución for the obligatory tourist selfie with the famous image of that murderous, racist, homophobic thug, Che Guevara. Images of the Argentinian-born "hero" of Cuba's revolution adorn merchandise around the globe. Whether a T-shirt or a hat, a coffee mug or a lighter, private enterprise has, in a wonderful irony, supplied unthinking leftists an endless supply of ways to wear Che's image.

Unfortunately for Cubans, Che wasn't nearly as good at planning production as capitalists have been at plastering his image on merchandise. During Che's stints as head of the National Bank of Cuba, minister of finance, and minister of industry, Cuba not only failed to industrialize (as promised), but its sugar production collapsed and severe rationing was introduced.

Che was a bad economist and an even worse humanitarian. He sent dissidents, homosexuals, Catholics, Jehovah's Witnesses, Afro-Cuban priests, and others he deemed undesirable to concentration camps where they were forced to do hard labor. When he ran the La Cabaña prison, he conducted sham military trials for "enemies of the revolution." The trials lacked any semblance of due process. The only court of appeal was Che, who never overturned a conviction. Estimates vary, but it is likely that when Che ran the prison in the first six months of 1959, up to five hundred people were executed.

Argentinians now have a phrase, "I have a Che T-shirt and I don't know why." That probably applies to most people wearing Che merchandise. The Che industry would collapse faster than a socialist economy if people bothered to learn about his murderous record.

We were walking up the grand steps of the impressive entrance to the university when a student stopped short and asked us, in perfect English, "Where are you from?"

"*¡Los Estados Unidos!*"

He smiled, shook our hands, and chatted with us. He was happy President Obama had visited Cuba, and said something that neither one of us will ever forget:

"I am glad you Americans are coming, because you bring us more money."

Only that's *not* what he said. That's what we expected him to say, and we wouldn't have faulted him if he had. Who doesn't want more money? What he actually said was even better:

"I am glad you Americans are coming, because you bring us more *freedom*."

As economists, we believe that the American government's half-century-long embargo on Cuba is bad policy, and that without it, we could bring the Cubans *more* freedom. The embargo has done nothing to undermine Cuba's abusive Communist regime. Indeed, the Castros have used the embargo—they call it a "blockade"—to blame the United States for Cuba's poverty rather than admit that socialism doesn't work. Trade not only promotes economic development, it can open a society to other ideas—in this case, capitalist ones.

Economists Peter Leeson, Russell Sobel, and Andrea Dean call this phenomenon "contagious capitalism."[6] They studied changes in economic freedom in one hundred countries during the period from 1985 to 2000. They were especially interested in whether economic policy changes in one country would lead to similar changes among its geographically closest trading partners. And, indeed, the answer was yes—economic freedom is contagious and spreads from freer countries to their less free trading partners.

That young Cuban's optimism and desire for freedom made us more hopeful about the prospects for reform.

After we landed in Miami, Bob asked, "Do you smell that?"

"Smell what?"

"It's the smell of freedom."

And it was. Relatively speaking.

* * *

A few months later there was another smell in the air. It was flavor. We were in Little Havana, in Miami. The economic contrast between Little Havana and the real thing began before we even stepped out of our Uber. The half-hour car ride cost us only $13.72 instead of the absurd taxi costs in Cuba. The visual contrast started the moment we stepped out of the car. Signs. They were everywhere. A cartoon of a cigar-smoking chicken advertised the Little Havana Gift Shop. Unlike stores in Cuba, this store had hundreds of different items for sale. And that's just what I could see from the door. I hate tacky gift shops.

Bob pointed behind us towards a sign for a bar. "Let's get a cold drink."

The mojitos tasted the same as they did in Cuba. Bob's colleague Daniel was with us. He ordered a meat and cheese platter and it was obvious when it came that the selection wasn't limited by a state-run supply chain.

"Mmm. This is *real* serrano ham! Not that prosciutto crap people try to pass off." Daniel was born in Mexico and is of Basque-Spanish descent, and he is unusually opinionated about such matters. Neither of us gringos would know the difference between serrano and prosciutto, but even we could tell the difference between this delicious plate and the minced meat product we'd seen in Cuba.

After a few rounds we headed off to a Cuban restaurant for dinner. The six-page menu contained more options than we had seen from all of the restaurants in Cuba combined. Bob and I were tempted by the mouthwatering selection of Cuban sandwiches, but we decided that as a matter of science we should order something we ate in Cuba.

Bob had the *ropa vieja,* and I had a lobster tail. Both had more flavor and spices than we had encountered in Cuba. Unfortunately, that didn't stop us envying the ham, pork, and cheese sandwich that Daniel was eating.

Cuban cuisine is excellent—just not when it's served in Cuba. It's not the Cubans' fault. It's the fact that socialism sucks.

Cubans under a socialist system remain poor and eat bland food. Ninety miles away, Cubans who live in Miami become relatively rich and make wonderful food. Same people, two different economic systems, two drastically different economic—and gastronomic—outcomes.

CHAPTER THREE

DARK SOCIALISM: NORTH KOREA

MAY 2017

We stood on the promenade along the Chinese side of the Yalu River, which separates the People's Republic of China from the Democratic People's Republic of Korea. Lights glimmered and neon signs flashed from the high-rises that loomed along the Chinese side of the river. But when we gazed into North Korea, there was nothing, nada, zilch. There was only pure darkness, even though the moon was shining brightly. Supposedly Sinuiju, a North Korean city populated by more than 350,000 people, and one of the country's most important trade hubs with China, lay in that darkness on the other side.[1]

We had just had dinner in the Koreatown neighborhood of Dandong with documentary filmmaker Dean Peng, who not only shared our passion for hard-core libertarian economics but had also volunteered to act as our translator and fixer in China. (We had been introduced by our mutual friend Li Schoolland, a Chinese-born free market advocate now living in Hawaii.) We had hoped to talk with émigré North Koreans, but that proved difficult. Our young North Korean waitress of Chinese parentage, for instance, had recently emigrated because she wanted a better life than was possible in North Korea, but she was quick to add that North Korea wasn't as bad as some people said. When she talked about North Korea she practically shook with fear, as if worried that any criticism would get her in trouble. Respecting that, we didn't press her for more information.

Of course, as a child of two Chinese parents, she was one of the lucky ones. Most native North Koreans who escape to China are captured by the Chinese authorities and returned to North Korea, where they might be executed and their families sent to hard labor camps.[2]

The ones who do escape successfully often go through harrowing ordeals. We were familiar with Yeonmi Park's book *In Order to Live: A North Korean Girl's Journey to Freedom*.[3] She had escaped to China when she was thirteen, but her smugglers raped her and told her she would either be sold to sex traffickers or returned to North Korea. She escaped both fates and was a fugitive in China for two years before she found Christian missionaries who smuggled her to safety in Mongolia.

So we understood why people like our waitress might not be so talkative.

After dinner, we strolled the promenade along the river, but there wasn't much going on. I saw one strip club and suggested we investigate. Dean didn't think it was a good idea. We've been to our fair share of strip clubs around the world, and usually have no moral reservations about visiting one. The vast majority of strippers choose to work in clubs because it's their best option for making money, and we have no problem helping them in that endeavor. But there, on the North Korean border, we did have reservations. Many North Korean refugees are coerced with the threat of deportation if they don't agree to work in the Chinese sex industry. Although I was interested to see what the club was like, and to see if we could learn anything from refugees, we ultimately wanted no part in propping up the traffickers, so we heeded Dean's advice and walked on.

The next morning, when we opened the curtains in our room on the twenty-first floor of our hotel, we were surprised by Sinuiju. Invisible the night before, daylight revealed dozens upon dozens of mid-rise commercial, industrial, and residential buildings just across the river. They weren't nearly as numerous, nice, or tall as the ones in Dandong. But still, ten-story, semi-dilapidated buildings were plentiful.

The view of North Korea (upper left) across the river from Dandong, China, is almost completely dark at night, while the Chinese side is aglow.

Same view in the morning: the North Korean side reveals itself to be a city of small buildings with little sign of life compared to the busy Chinese city. But unlike at night, at least you can tell it is there.

We'd come to Dandong to get a closer look at North Korea, but our adventure had started about a week earlier in Seoul, South Korea. The Korean peninsula is a rare natural experiment where capitalism and socialism can be compared side by side. The comparison is particularly informative because North and South Korea share a common history, language, culture, and, before they split, level of economic development.

The North is a bit colder and more mountainous, but those differences hadn't disproportionately hindered development in the North before the split. At the end of World War II, North Korea had about 80 percent of Korea's industry, 90 percent of its electrical power, and 75 percent of its mines: iron, tungsten, silver, and uranium.[4]

The Korean War left the entire peninsula devastated. Perhaps the North suffered greater losses, but it quickly rebuilt with Soviet military and economic aid. It's impossible to accurately measure incomes in socialist countries, because they lack meaningful prices, but by most accounts, average GDP per capita was roughly the same between the North and South in 1960.

The most significant difference was that North Korea was a Communist state with a socialist economic system, while South Korea was an authoritarian but eventually democratic state with a capitalist economic system.

In North Korea, all private businesses and industries were eliminated by the late 1950s, and private agriculture was largely abolished and replaced with collectivization, where farmers grow produce for state warehouses that then distribute the food.[5] North Korea followed a Soviet model of development, focusing its economy on heavy industry and the military. It is also a totalitarian police state enforcing the most thoroughgoing socialist economic system in the world.

South Korea, by contrast, is basically capitalist. In Bob's economic freedom index, South Korea scores 7.54 out of 10 points. That leaves it less economically free than top-rated Hong Kong (8.97) and the eleventh-ranked United States (7.94). But this still leaves it in the top 80th percentile of countries scored. From the moment we landed, South Korea was impressive. We breezed through Incheon International Airport, which had been ranked as the best global airport for nine consecutive years (through 2013) by the Airports Council International. Even the immigration and customs process, which usually royally pisses Bob and me off, was only a minor annoyance. We were in a modern Kia taxi and headed into Seoul in no time, darting through relatively light Saturday afternoon traffic. Glancing out the windows, we saw Seoul's hills and valleys covered in modern buildings.

After the long flight from Dallas, we wanted to get onto Korean time right away. To us, that means getting drunk and passing out at the local bedtime. In addition to researching this book, Bob and I were also speaking at another meeting of the Mont Pelerin Society, and some of our friends had already arrived. After checking in, we met up with our bald, cigar-smoking drinking buddy and raconteur of raunchy jokes, Steve Gohmann, who runs the Center for Free Enterprise at the University of Louisville.

We found a great Korean barbeque with delicious pork belly and kimchi and ended up smoking cigars outside a Belgian beer bar. Despite being on the opposite side of the planet from where they were brewed, the beers were cheaper than in high-tax Sweden, which meant we would buy more of them, and Belgian beers have around double the alcohol content of American lagers, so we succeeded in adjusting to local time quite rapidly.

Seoul is massive. Its total economic output ranks it fourth in the world among metropolitan areas (behind Tokyo, New York, and Los Angeles). Fifteen Fortune Global 500 companies, including Samsung, LG, and Hyundai-Kia, have their headquarters in Seoul. Its more than twenty-five million people live well too. Average incomes, adjusted for cost-of-living differences, amount to more than $42,000. It's hard to get an accurate picture of a country's economy without looking beyond its capital city. But in South Korea's case, average incomes in Seoul are only about $5,000 higher than the national average.[6]

Since 1960, South Korea has rocketed from a pre-industrial standard of living to being a wealthy first-world country. Life expectancy has improved from fifty-three to eighty-two years.

Infant mortality is now just three deaths per 100,000, down from eighty-one in 1960, a whopping 96 percent reduction! Incomes have more than tripled after adjusting for inflation.[7] Virtually everything has improved.

That night when I stumbled back into my hotel room after drinking with Bob and Steve, I encountered a problem: The toilet had more buttons than my iPhone's home screen. There were buttons with butt cheeks and dashed lines of spray, a girl's face, a dryer, a bathtub, a child, hi, low, front, back, water, light, seat, and more. The last time I'd tried to use a similar computerized toilet in Tokyo, I got cornholed with scalding water. I made the only sensible choice. I pissed in the shower and went to bed. But capitalism has done pretty well for Seoul if this is the worst we encountered.

Seoul is only 35 miles from the North Korean border. The 1953 cease-fire after the Korean War established a 2.5-mile-wide demilitarized zone (DMZ) all along the 160-mile border to serve as a buffer between the countries. We joined our fellow conference attendees for one of the standard tours along the DMZ. Most Americans who want to see North Korea do so on one of these tours, but unfortunately, there isn't much to see. It was a gloomy and foggy day, so we used tourist binoculars to see across the Han River and the DMZ into North Korea. Only a couple of small farming villages and isolated homes were visible in the distance. This was no way to gauge how North Koreans lived or how their economy operated.

Ideally, we'd fly to Pyongyang, the North Korean capital, and then travel around the country a bit and observe what we could. But North Korea allows U.S. tourists into only carefully controlled staged areas within the capital city. Tourists are constantly accompanied and monitored by government employees. Traveling freely and observing normal people is not an option.

Even with those limitations, we might have done the official tour, but for two things: We doubted the North Koreans would grant us visas, given our outspoken opposition to Communism, and to be honest I didn't want to go. I've read horror stories of visiting missionaries getting ten years of hard labor for having a sermon on a USB drive. A little over a year before our trip Otto Warmbier, a college student from Bob's hometown of Cincinnati, who had gone on one of the official tours, was sentenced to fifteen years in prison doing hard labor for allegedly stealing a single propaganda poster. About a month after our trip he was returned to the United States having been beaten into a coma; he died not long after. I think we had good reason not to trust the North Korean government.

So that's how we chose Dandong, China, where we'd be able to get a much closer look into North Korea and talk to some people, like our waitress, who had lived there.

Along the promenade, numerous Chinese boats offered river tours. Chinese tourists are just as fascinated to peer into the hermit kingdom as we were. We took two trips with official tour vessels— one trip downriver to see the commercial and industrial part of Sinuiju, and another upriver to see residential areas and the rural outskirts.

We were wary of the sketchy boat captains who offered to take us up one of the small tributaries into North Korea proper, where we could trade money with North Koreans for trinkets and other souvenirs. We figured the captains must bribe the North Korean army officers to look the other way while they bring in Chinese tourists. It was probably safe, but there was no guarantee that they wouldn't hand us over to North Korean soldiers in return for a bounty for capturing American "spies."

At one point, our commercial tour boat passed under the Sino-Korean Friendship Bridge. While we saw some occasional rail traffic passing across the bridge during our stay, nothing could pass over the neighboring bridge about fifty yards downriver. Supposedly, the North Korean government had never repaired the "Broken Bridge" after the war because it didn't want the United States to be able to deny bombing it. The Chinese have no such reservations, and now tourists stroll out on the repaired half of the bridge for a better look into North Korea.

Industrial buildings and shipping yards stretch along the North Korean riverbank, but they aren't much to look at. They're mostly one- or two-story structures of pale beige or concrete gray, with an occasional bright green building mixed in, with trucks and small shipping cranes scattered among them. Some of the workers who were easily visible from our boat were busy loading the gray barges tied up to shore, while others sat idle.

Bob pointed out several Chinese Coast Guard boats cruising along the river in our immediate proximity. "Never thought I'd be happy to see the Chinese Navy." I agreed. If our little boat broke down, we sure as hell wanted the Chinese Coast Guard picking us up before our American asses washed up on the North Korean shore.

We noticed a large Ferris wheel and what appeared to be an amusement park waterslide just before we turned around and headed back to the dock. The Ferris wheel wasn't moving, and the place looked overgrown with brush and trees. It's easily visible from the river promenade, and none of the locals had ever seen it move. Maybe it's there to convince the Chinese tourists that North Koreans are having a good time.

The boat trip upriver was even more depressing. Dilapidated, beige, two-story concrete apartment homes with semi-caved-in orange-tiled roofs clung to the shore. Dingy smoke billowed from behind one row of them. A few people washed clothes in the river while others fished. Farther on, the river splits multiple times, and there are farms and smaller towns where the bright blue military guard towers identify the North Korean bank and islands. The river is quite narrow in places and it would be easy, if not for minefields and guard towers, for North Koreans to swim across into China.

We saw poverty in North Korea, but it was nothing new to us. We've both traveled to many poor countries. Average incomes in North Korea today are estimated at around $1,700, though even that number is almost certainly bullshit.[8] The country's capital stock is in disrepair, shortages are frequent, and Koreans have even suffered starvation.

Estimates vary widely since accurate data aren't available, but in the 1990s, when Soviet and Chinese aid decreased, up to three million North Koreans died of starvation and related diseases. Food shortages still remain a problem. When Yeonmi Park escaped North Korea, she was astonished to be given "a whole bowl of rice and some spicy pickled cucumber. . .I had never seen a cucumber in winter." She added that her trafficker threw away more food in his garbage than she might eat in a week in North Korea.[9]

North Korea remains among the poorest countries in the world, but their material poverty isn't much worse than what we've seen in other parts of Asia or Africa. What is shocking is the contrast between North Korea and its neighbors, China and South Korea. We stood on a riverboat with dilapidated two-story decaying housing and poverty on one side of us, and just a few hundred yards across the river there were glistening high-rises and Chinese citizens enjoying a first-world standard of living.

At one point, we saw a lone North Korean farmer on a tractor pulling a plow through a field. This was unusual, because thus far we'd seen peasants farming only with animals and hand tools. The ancient diesel engine strained as the tractor tried to get up a slight incline, and after a few minutes of battling, the poor farmer gave up and let the tractor roll backward. It was a stark contrast between this man's situation and the semi-trailer trucks that flew down the highway on the Chinese side of the river at sixty miles an hour. These differences are not natural; they are entirely driven by the different economic systems of North Korea and China.

The side-by-side contrast between North and South Korea is even greater. Their economic systems are even more different from each other's than North Korea's and China's are, but the contrast is hard to see from the ground because of the DMZ and the lack of cities directly next to each other. You can, however, see it from space.

Nighttime satellite images reveal South Korea lit up like a Christmas tree, with a massive star of light emanating from Seoul, and lesser filaments of light flowing all across the country. Except for a small dot of light in Pyongyang and narrow stretches of light spilling across the Yalu River in China, the North is dark. Nowhere on earth is the contrast between socialism and capitalism as black and white—or, in this case, black and light—as it is here.

CHAPTER FOUR

FAKE SOCIALISM: CHINA

MAY 2017

It was obvious that China wasn't a socialist country before our plane even landed in Beijing. Tall buildings, some of them skyscrapers, stretched for miles in multiple directions and didn't have the uniform bland gray exteriors that typify socialist architecture. Heights, shapes, materials, and designs all varied. These initial impressions held as our modern taxi cab whisked us down the crowded but efficiently flowing ten-lane highway towards downtown. Not only were these modern buildings well maintained and varied, but they also bore telltale signs of capitalism—company names and logos.

We could have stayed in many great five-star hotels run by international companies in Beijing. But that would have been like staying in the Hotel Nacional in Havana and using that one experience to generalize about the other hotels. So, as in Cuba, we shot for decent hotels at reasonable prices. Only in China there was one major difference—our hotels didn't totally suck.

The twenty-story Novotel Beijing Peace Hotel boasted four hundred rooms and contained Le Cabernet, a French restaurant, as well as another restaurant serving mixed international cuisine. The lobby bar was fully stocked, and I could order my standard double gin and tonics for around ten bucks each. The guest rooms were unremarkable, which is to say, nice. If you were just dropped into one of them, without knowing anything else, you'd probably guess you were in a Marriott or Sheraton hotel in the United States. In fact, if it wasn't for the trinkets in the gift shops and all the Chinese people walking around, nothing in the hotel indicated we were in China at all.

That's no accident. Novotel is part of the French multinational AccorHotels group. The Novotel chain has about four hundred hotels in sixty countries. It's also privately owned, so it depends on customers' purchases to stay in business. But we weren't breaking the bank to buy luxury in a socialist country. Our reservation cost us $106 per night and we were about a kilometer from the city center, within easy walking distance of the Forbidden City and Tiananmen Square. Well, it was easy for Bob at least. I was hobbling with a cane because I had semi-drunkenly broken my big toe while wearing flip-flops in Hawaii three weeks prior.

We had a few hours to kill before we met Dean Peng, who was going to help us find our way around China, so we decided to wander the neighborhood and get a beer. We were surrounded—engulfed is probably the better word—in capitalist commerce. Signs were everywhere, and they were signs we recognized: Rolex, Gap, McDonald's, and Pizza Hut.

Just off the main street, Bob and I bobbed and weaved our way through crowded, narrow alleys where mom-and-pop small businesses sold silks, toys, and fried scorpion on a stick. We were relieved to find a bar with a couple of seats open. They were selling Tsingtao beer, oversized, and properly overpriced.

We were surrounded by free-market commerce in the capital of Communist China, which for nearly thirty years, under dictator Mao Zedong, had been one of the most repressive regimes in the world. As Chairman of China's Communist Party, Mao ruled the "People's Republic" from its founding in October 1949 until his death in 1976. His rule was near absolute. Party officials who dared to challenge him lost their jobs—or worse. Party members and peasants alike were expected to study his writings, including his "Little Red Book" of political and economic philosophy. As fake as the country's socialism is now, the Communist Party still runs China, and children are still taught to revere "Chairman Mao," almost certainly the biggest mass murderer in history.

Frank Dikötter, in his book *Mao's Great Famine*, estimates that at least forty-five million people died unnecessarily in China between 1958 and 1962 alone. The great famine did not occur because of a drought or natural disaster; it occurred because of Mao's economic plan for industrialization.

Mao's inspiration was Soviet leader Nikita Khrushchev's 1957 promise that the Soviet Union would overtake the economic production of the United States within fifteen years. Mao responded that China would grow even more rapidly. His first goal was for China to overtake the economic output of Great Britain, and the result was his ambitious plan—called the Great Leap Forward—for the Communist government to industrialize China.

The Great Leap Forward became the great Chinese famine. But as Dikötter explains, referring to this tragedy as a mere famine "fails to capture the many ways in which people died under radical collectivization. The blithe use of the term 'famine' also lends support to the widespread view that these deaths were the unintended consequence of half-baked and poorly executed economic programmes." In fact, "coercion, terror, and systematic violence were the foundations of the Great Leap Forward."[1] The Great Leap Forward could not even be justified under the usual socialist excuse of breaking a few eggs to create an omelet. In reality, it was a Great Leap Backward, killing tens of millions of people and destroying, rather than modernizing, China's economy.

The government was already seizing small, family-run farms and moving the farmers into government-run "cooperatives" of about a thousand workers each. In 1958, Mao doubled down and merged the cooperatives into giant "people's communes" that could incorporate as many as twenty thousand households. Party officials ran the communes, where nearly everything—land, tools, livestock—was collectivized. Millions upon millions of villagers were forcibly moved to make way for giant damming and other projects. Targets were set—and escalated—for communes to export not just food but also industrial products, such as steel. Backyard furnaces soon melted down pots, pans, farming tools, and anything else that was available to meet the quotas. To feed his cities and meet foreign export promises, Mao continued to demand more and more from the farmers, even as able-bodied farm workers were diverted to projects the planners cared more about, like building dams. The result was agricultural failure, famine (some of it implemented by commune leaders to motivate workers), and steel production (melted down scrap metal from backyard furnaces) that was economically useless.

Dikötter's examination of Chinese Communist Party records shows that at least two and a half million people were summarily executed or tortured to death during the Great Leap Forward. Millions more starved because they were intentionally deprived of food as punishment, or because they were regarded as too old or weak to be productive, or because the people ladling out the slop in the chow line simply did not like them.

Our friend Li Schoolland remembered that during the later years of the Great Leap Forward, "We ate everything that didn't kill us. I refused to eat rats. But my brother, he was a growing boy. He was so hungry. He ate it. We'd go to the pond and get the snails and the frogs." Her family also ate "tree bark, tree leaves, grass, I knew all the grass that was edible."[2]

Mao received many reports of starvation and suffering, but he and the Communist Party were unmoved. In late 1958 Mao's foreign minister, Chen Yi, acknowledged that "casualties have indeed appeared among workers, but it is not enough to stop us in our tracks. This is a price we have to pay, it's nothing to be afraid of. Who knows how many people have been sacrificed on the battlefields and in the prisons [for the revolutionary cause]? Now we have a few cases of illness and death: It's nothing!"[3] Eventually, however, the Communist Party had to relent in order to avoid complete catastrophe as the tens of millions of casualties piled up. By 1962, the Great Leap Forward had been abandoned, and some private farmland had been reintroduced. But it was a short-lived respite. In 1966, Mao and the Communist Party launched the "Cultural Revolution," inflicting a new hell on the Chinese people.

The Cultural Revolution aimed to purge or reeducate the counterrevolutionary bourgeois elements of Chinese society. It also served to reassert Mao's power after the failure of the Great Leap Forward. Senior officials, including the future reformer Deng Xiaoping, were purged from leadership in the Communist Party. Historical sites and relics that honored things from China's pre-Communist past were destroyed. Roughly seventeen million young people were sent to the rural countryside for class reeducation.[4] Other young people formed the Red Guard and attacked anyone insufficiently supportive of Maoism. The death toll of the Cultural Revolution is estimated at somewhere between half a million and two million people.[5]

All told, in less than thirty years, through the Great Leap Forward, the Cultural Revolution, and other atrocities, Mao's Communist government killed more of its own people than any other government in history—possibly as many as eighty million.[6] The peasants who escaped death found themselves poorer than their ancestors. In 1978, two-thirds of Chinese peasants had incomes lower than they had in the 1950s, one-third had incomes lower than in the 1930s, and the average Chinese person was only consuming two-thirds as many calories as the average person in a developed country.[7]

But none of this suffering was obvious from where we stood now in Tiananmen Square. Rather than starving peasants, we were surrounded by Chinese tourists sporting digital cameras, cell phones, and shopping bags. The Communist Party continues to govern China, but it has allowed free-market reforms that have delivered prosperity.

If this was obvious in Beijing, it was even more obvious in our next stop—Shanghai. The Shanghai Tower—2,073 feet and 127 stories tall—is the second-tallest building in the world. Its observation deck, complete with beer-serving café, afforded us a 360-degree bird's-eye view of countless high-rises along both banks of the Huangpu River, a tributary of the Yangtze. The river itself was chock-full of barges serving the world's busiest container port. It's hard to decide what counts as a high-rise in Shanghai. There were far more thirty-story buildings than I could count. Even limiting myself to the forty- or fifty-story buildings would have been dizzying, especially after I'd consumed a few of the café's beers. Nearly next door to the Shanghai Tower, the nine-year-old Shanghai World Financial Center stands at 101 stories and 1,614 feet. Not far beyond that is Shanghai's iconic 1,535-foot-tall Oriental Pearl Tower. Completed in 1994, the Pearl is the oldest of Shanghai's mega skyscrapers.

In fact, nearly everything on the east side of the river was new. As recently as 1990, this area, known as Pudong, had been a slum. But in less than a generation those slums were replaced by mega skyscrapers, shopping outlets, a financial district, and high-end hotels. In fact, I wish we had stayed in one of those hotels. Instead, after SMU's travel agency screwed up our reservations, Bob booked us last-minute at the Hotel Ibis, another AccorHotels property, across the river in old Shanghai's historical center. And it sucked. Not Cuba suck. More like wet-dog smell, shitty AC, no bar or mini bar, Motel 6, American-variety suck. Oh well, capitalism usually provides, but even capitalism can't always overcome problems stemming from university bureaucracies.

Ben takes a break from drinking with Bob's SMU students in definitely not-socialist Shanghai. The Pudong district across the river behind him was a slum before 1993, when it became a special economic zone with greater economic freedoms and immediately began transforming into the rich, developed city you see here.

China's economic development since 1978 is one of the greatest successes of its kind in human history. In sheer numbers, more people have escaped from extreme poverty, defined as earning less than two dollars a day, than at any other time or place. In 2011, 750 million fewer Chinese lived in absolute poverty than in 1981. Their living standards improved dramatically because the Chinese Communist Party adopted free-market policies.

The reforms started slowly, with collectivized farms contracting land to farmers who could sell their surplus (after they met their quotas) on private markets. The government recognized that farmers free to make profits were more productive. Instead of following their Communist ideology, government bureaucrats finally accepted the facts and allowed increasing degrees of private property.

Private enterprise was, in part, an unexpected by-product of the seventeen million Chinese young people who returned to the cities after their forced rural reeducation at the end of the Cultural Revolution. They needed jobs that inefficient, state-owned industries couldn't provide—so self-employment became legal, as did small private businesses. By law, such businesses could only employ up to seven people, but in practice, by 1985, the average private company in China employed thirty people.[8]

Under the leadership of Deng Xiaoping, the Communist Party made effective economic development, rather than ideological purity, the focus of government policy, claiming, "It doesn't matter whether the cat is black or white, as long as it catches mice." No surprise to us, the more capitalist the cat, the more effective it was at catching mice. Deng defined his policy as "market socialism with Chinese characteristics," which really was hardly socialism at all.

Bob had tracked China's development with his economic freedom index. In 1980, the first year for which he had reliable data, China scored only 3.64 out of 10, placing it at the bottom 10 percent of countries in the world. By 1990, China's economic freedom score had jumped 75 percent to 6.40. In 1988, the Chinese constitution was amended to officially recognize private property and private business. Before then, the Communist state had been China's only official employer, with small exceptions. By 1998, the state employed about 60 percent of the working population, and in 2010 it employed only about 19 percent.[9] China had transitioned from socialism to a form of crony capitalism.

Bob recited all these statistics at a fancy bar, holding court to a group of his SMU MBA students we had literally just chanced upon. They listened politely and then bought us a round of shots, hoping we'd take the hint and leave. We did, stumbling our way along the Bund, a riverfront walkway through the old colonial concessions to the British, American, and French governments that had opened up Shanghai as an international trade port in the nineteenth century. Across the river, the Pudong skyline glowed a brilliant blue, pink, red, purple, white, and gold. I gestured drunkenly in its direction and told Bob, "You know, your index misses a lot of that."

That's because Bob's index measures policies mostly at the national level, so it can underestimate the contribution of a place like Pudong, which is a special economic zone (SEZ) with certain commercial privileges. Shanghai and thirteen other cities became SEZs in 1984, and Pudong became one in 1993. Special economic zones pay no customs duties on internationally traded goods, are exempt from income taxes, and have a host of other pro-capitalism rules that the rest of China hasn't yet adopted.

Pudong is also included in the Lujiazui Finance and Trade Zone, which grants additional freedoms to foreign financial institutions and banks. This is a major advantage, because the Chinese government monopolizes the finance industry in most of the country. Pudong also includes the Waigaoqiao Free Trade Zone, which, at about four square miles, is the largest free trade zone in mainland China.

The economic freedom granted in SEZs has fueled much of China's growth. Today, in Pudong, annual incomes average more than $20,000. Yet, according to the World Bank, throughout the rest of the country more than a third of Chinese people still live on less than $5.50 a day. Meanwhile, the population of Shanghai has exploded from eleven million people in 1980 to more than twenty-four million. Its population density is nearly three times that of Beijing, which has also seen its population surge.

In fact, the massive movement of people from low-productivity rural areas to cities with private industry has spurred China's development. In the years since reform began, more than 260 million migrants moved from rural areas to urban centers in China, helping to transform China from a rural, socialist hellhole to an increasingly urbanized, mostly capitalist country. But on our trip we were reminded that, politically at least, China is still a Communist police state.

In Beijing, Bob and I had been invited by a young Chinese scholar, Ma Junjie, to speak at a conference about Austrian economics and the author Ayn Rand. The conference was organized by Unirule—an influential, private, free-market, Chinese think tank—and our friend, Yaron Brook, who runs the Ayn Rand Institute.

Yaron is a gray-haired former-finance-professor-turned-philosopher who travels the world evangelizing for the ideas of Ayn Rand. In attendance were about thirty Chinese academics, graduate students, think-tank scholars, and journalists. Discussing the ideas of novelist Ayn Rand, one of the most ardent anti-Communists of the twentieth century, while in the heart of Beijing was pretty damned surreal for us, but we did our best, participating on a panel discussion about Austrian economics and Ayn Rand's philosophy of objectivism.

A couple of conference attendees drove us to dinner afterwards. As it happened, our route took us by Mao's mausoleum. The fellow in the passenger seat turned around to us, nodded toward the massive complex, and said, "Maybe in twenty-five years we can get rid of him." The driver laughed and shouted, "No! Ten years!" In China, this is risky talk.

The next day, after we had departed for Shanghai, Li School-land sent us an email: "I hope you didn't go to the Unirule event yesterday!"

Using our VPN-equipped cell phones, we circumvented Chinese government censorship and accessed the internet. The *South China Morning Post* reported, "A two-day academic seminar at China's largest non-official think tank was called off on Saturday because doors and lifts at its office building were locked and disabled amid upgraded security for Beijing's two-day belt and road forum that begins on Sunday."[10]

Li's second email provided more details. "Yesterday before the meeting, the government blockaded the building where Unirule's office is located and hired some thugs to beat up people who tried to enter. So the event had to cancel. Very bad situation and dangerous." We also discovered that Unirule's founder, eighty-eight-year-old Mao Yushi, who has received the prestigious international Milton Friedman Prize for Advancing Liberty, had police officers arrive at his house that morning to prevent him from leaving for the conference.

Bob nerds out to Ayn Rand at the Unirule Institute meeting in Beijing. The meeting would be shut down by the government the very next morning.

Since our departure, Communist Party leader Xi Jinping has continued his crackdown on dissent, and on Unirule. The government shut down Unirule's websites and social media accounts and forced the institute to vacate its downtown offices that we had visited. Unirule moved to western Beijing, put up a website accessible only to those with VPN software, and was continually harassed.[11] In July 2018, the building landlord evicted Unirule, though the institute had always paid its bills. The institute's executive director, Sheng Hong, explained, "The leasing company is out to make money, and there's no reason that they'd make trouble on their own. That would be illogical."[12] Instead, Sheng explained, "It must be the pressure from the government. The authorities do not want [to tolerate] a different voice, but they do not want to brazenly shut us down either, because that would make it look too terrible." Instead, "They obviously want to try to turn it into a civil dispute, but people are not idiots and everyone can tell what's the real matter here."[13]

When Communist China was governed by socialist ideologues it was an impoverished, totalitarian police state that killed tens of millions of its own people. Now that Communist China practices crony capitalism, it is a prosperous and much more restrained police state. That sucks, but believe us—that's still progress.

CHAPTER FIVE

HUNGOVER SOCIALISM: RUSSIA & UKRAINE

SEPTEMBER 2017

"This looks like any European city," Bob said as we walked around central Moscow on an overcast, drizzly afternoon in late September. Expensive cars darted about the streets past a mix of modern glass-and-stone structures and renovated pre-Soviet buildings. The plain, gray, Soviet block-housing that many people called home in the days of the Soviet Union and Eastern Bloc were noticeably absent.

Shops were plentiful and well stocked. There was no shortage of bars, and the restaurants boasted varied cuisine, like in any major city. We had just left the Tap and Barrel Pub, an Irish joint, where we'd enjoyed a pint of Kilkenny. Try finding that in Havana or Pyongyang.

The Soviet Union broke apart politically in 1991, and after twenty-six years of reform, we can tell you that failed socialism in Moscow looks pretty unremarkable. If you closed your eyes and opened them quickly, you might think you were in Stockholm, Warsaw, or Berlin, until the onion dome spires of St. Basil's Cathedral give away your location.

The remaining evidence of Soviet times is mostly monuments and images, like the aging art deco mural featuring a muscular Soviet cosmonaut painted on the side of a building. We're not art critics, but all the bulging muscles in socialist art look like soft-core gay porn to us. However, there was nothing soft-core about the statue we encountered a little farther down the street, where a fourteen-foot-tall bust of Karl Marx rose out of a large gray block of stone.

Marx wasn't the first socialist thinker, but he was certainly the most influential. His ideas inspired the movements that would ultimately establish the Soviet Union, China's Communist government, and numerous other socialist regimes in the twentieth century. His ideas appealed to labor activists in his own lifetime and continue to influence leftist intellectuals and young socialists. Che might outsell Marx in T-shirts, but Marx is quoted far more often than Che in university lecture halls.

Tons of books have been written on Marx, and we don't want to bore you here by going through his entire life and work, but it's worth at least briefly reviewing his ideas on value, alienation, and history, the three big pillars of Marxism.

Even though we're free-market economists, Marx's labor theory of value doesn't offend us. He was wrong, but it wasn't until after Marx died that economists figured it out. Most economists, including the great classical liberal, Adam Smith, were mistaken in their labor, or cost-of-production, theory of value. It wasn't until the so-called "Marginal Revolution" in the 1880s when three economists, working independently, all concluded that the value of a good is based on what people subjectively think a particular (or "marginal") unit of that good is worth, which is exactly right. The amount of time or energy it takes to make something doesn't really matter when it comes to determining its worth. This is tough to grasp, especially for the individuals or company that produced the good and want to sell it for a price that they think is "fair" compensation for their time and labor. But stick with us here and we'll explain.

A good's worth is entirely in the eye of the beholder. It might cost six times as much to produce an orange in a greenhouse in Alaska as it does to grow one outside in Florida, but Alaskan oranges are no more valuable to consumers than Floridian oranges. Costs, whether labor or otherwise, just tell us whether it makes sense to produce something a particular way *given* the value we expect people will pay for the good that is produced.

Marx, like most of his contemporaries, mistakenly thought the amount of labor "embodied" in a good was what determined its value. He claimed that if labor determines value, then any profits made by a capitalist must represent exploitation, because workers must not have received the full value of the good that they created.

A separate, though related, aspect of Marx's thought is alienation. Workers are alienated because market forces, not the workers themselves, decide what will be produced, how it will be produced, and who will produce it.

This means that workers are forced to work for the capitalists who own the means of production and dictate terms to the workers, often leaving them in dull, monotonous jobs, earning unfair wages. Marx claimed that once private property in the means of production was eliminated, workers could produce for their needs, rather than for the capitalists' profits, and thus end alienation.

Marx's theory of history was the final pillar of his system. He believed the collapse of capitalism and transition to socialism was inevitable. His brand of "scientific socialism" dictated that history is a series of struggles between the privileged and exploited classes. Under capitalism, the bourgeoisie (the property-owning middle class) exploited the proletariat (the workers). Marx believed that capitalist competition would inevitably lead to financial losses, business failures, and then monopoly, and that as industries became more concentrated, many of the former bourgeoisie would be forced into the exploited proletariat. This would further depress wages and increase alienation. Ultimately, the masses would overthrow the capitalists and collectivize the means of production.

As we paused to look at the statue Bob said, "I bet there's never been a guy who has been so wrong about every major thing he wrote about and who still has as many followers as Marx." Bob's right. Profits don't represent exploitation, because the labor theory of value is wrong. Instead, at least in a free market, profits represent created value. Capitalism can't be the cause of alienation because workers inevitably do better under capitalism than under socialism, and market prices provide a higher standard of living and more economic opportunity. Finally, industries haven't become more concentrated and wages haven't been pushed down under capitalism. Instead, capitalism has been the engine of prosperity, innovation, new industries, and rising wages, while socialist economies have stagnated or even regressed.

"Yeah, there's only one great Marx," I said. "Groucho." Groucho's definition of politics is Marxism in a nutshell: "Politics is the art of looking for trouble, finding it everywhere, diagnosing it incorrectly, and applying the wrong remedies."

We continued our usual walk/drink/walk/drink routine until we reached Red Square. Growing up, this was the enemy's ground zero, and standing in Red Square felt odd. Saint Basil's dominated the far end of the square. To our right was the long red stone wall that encloses the Kremlin. The middle of Red Square was where the Soviet military paraded its might. Straight ahead, near the Kremlin wall, was the mausoleum of Vladimir Lenin, the first leader of the Soviet Union.

Many socialists today concede that Lenin's successor, Stalin, was a tyrant. But they often try to deflect blame from Lenin and socialism in general. The truth, however, is that Lenin was as evil as Stalin, just on a smaller scale. He was a dictator. He created the secret police, the Cheka, which would eventually become the KGB. He sent his political opponents to slave labor camps. He ordered mass executions and intentional mass starvation.

The Black Book of Communism, which details the many atrocities committed by socialist regimes, notes that it is "impossible to come up with an exact figure for the number of people who fell victim to this first great wave of the Red Terror.... [T]he total reported in the official press alone suggest that at the very least it must be between 10,000 and 15,000...summary executions in two months. In the space of a few weeks the Cheka alone had executed two to three times the total number of people condemned to death by the tsarist regime over ninety-two years."[1]

The Cossack people in southern Russia and southeastern Ukraine had opposed the Bolsheviks (the Communists) in the Russian Civil War and resisted Lenin's demands to give up their food and collectivize their farms. So Lenin embarked on a campaign to eliminate the Cossacks. They were classified as "kulaks" (a term for wealthier peasants) and "class enemies." *The Black Book* reports that "on the principle of collective responsibility, a new regime took a series of measures specially designed to eliminate, exterminate, and deport the population of a whole territory," and that these were not "heat of the battle decisions but planned by the highest authorities including Lenin."[2]

Land belonging to Cossacks was confiscated. The president of the Revolutionary Committee of the Don, who was in charge of imposing Bolshevik rule in Cossack territories, reported that "what was carried out...against the Cossacks was an indiscriminate policy of massive extermination."[3] Ultimately, "The Cossack regions of the Don and the Kuban paid a heavy price for their opposition to the Bolsheviks. According to the most reliable estimates, between 300,000 and 500,000 people were killed or deported in 1919 and 1920, out of a population of no more than three million."[4]

The great Russian famine of 1921 and 1922 was also largely Lenin's doing, as he requisitioned grain from peasant farmers who were left to starve. As reported in *The Black Book*, "Though perfectly well informed of the inevitable consequences of the requisitioning policy, the government took no steps to combat these predicted effects. On July 30, 1921, while famine gripped a growing number of regions, Lenin and Molotov sent a telegram to all leaders of regional and provincial Party committees asking them to 'bolster the mechanisms for food collection'" or, in other words, to press the farmers even harder.[5] Ultimately, at least five million people died during this man-made famine.

During the period known as War Communism, Lenin presided over a comprehensive program to nationalize the means of production. It was a disaster. Production plummeted, famine spread, and there were widespread revolts. Lenin ultimately introduced the

New Economic Policy (NEP), which was a step back from socialism, in 1921. It reintroduced money, legalized small-scale private industry, and allowed peasants to sell food on the open market. Socialist governments often bail themselves out with limited capitalist reforms before returning to their old ways, which is exactly what happened in 1928, when Stalin repealed the NEP.

With Lenin's mausoleum in front of us, Bob said, "Let's be tourists and go see the old bastard." After a long, socialist-style wait, we saw the murdering son of a bitch (who was also a prohibitionist—another reason to hate him) lying in a dimly lit room with Russian soldiers solemnly standing guard.[6] Visitors are supposed to walk slowly around the room in single file with heads down: no taking photographs, talking, smoking, wearing hats, or putting hands in pockets—so I put my hands in my pockets and got shouted at by a guard.

Lines were a fact of life in the Soviet Union. Communism may be gone in Moscow, but with zero-priced admission, lines still form for Lenin's tomb.

That was enough commie tourism for us. We moved along to the Hotel Metropol. The hotel, which opened in 1907, is a grand structure with beautifully ornate granite carvings, tiled images of princesses on its exterior, fine marble columns, and a stained glass skylight above the chandeliers in the lobby. Of course, the Bolsheviks nationalized it in 1918 and turned it into offices and living quarters for bureaucrats, but by the 1930s, they had converted it back to a hotel.

The Hotel Metropol was a big part of Moscow's Soviet history. S. J. Taylor, author of *Stalin's Apologist*, a scathing biography of *New York Times* reporter Walter Duranty, noted that "The *New York Times* man in Moscow could usually be found among the throngs at the bar of the Metropol Hotel."[7] In the early 1930s, the bar was the "focal point of a glittering bourgeois society in a dull setting of Proletarianism. It was little more than an alcove off the main dining room, yet sooner or later, practically every American who visited the Soviet Union made his way there."[8]

Not surprisingly, Bob and I found our way there too. It was still just a small rectangular bar in an alcove, but it was well stocked with vodka. We had a few and talked about how the *Times*, in its year-long series of columns on "The Red Century," never once mentioned how its own notorious Moscow correspondent in the 1920s and 1930s was a mere mouthpiece for Soviet propaganda.

Walter Duranty lived a privileged life in Moscow. He had a nice apartment, a car with a driver, a secretary, and could afford to eat and drink well and take frequent trips to Berlin, Paris, and St. Tropez. He was regarded as the leading foreign correspondent in Moscow, but far from being an honest, unbiased reporter, he saw his role as promoting the Communist regime.

Duranty won a Pulitzer Prize in 1932, with the prize committee praising him for his "scholarship, profundity, impartiality,
sound judgment, and exceptional clarity...."[9] In his acceptance
speech, Duranty stated that, "I discovered that the Bolsheviks were
sincere enthusiasts, trying to regenerate a people that had been
shockingly misgoverned, and I decided to try to give them their fair
break. I still believe they are doing the best for the Russian masses
and I believe in Bolshevism—for Russia." S. J. Taylor quotes
Duranty's approval of the "planned system of economy" and his
"respect" for "the Soviet leaders, especially Stalin, whom I consider
to have grown into a really great statesman."[10]

A year later, his admiration for Stalin and the Bolsheviks would
lead him to cover up what was, perhaps, the greatest atrocity Stalin
committed. After repealing the NEP, Stalin redoubled efforts to
collectivize farmland. Peasant farmers understandably resisted,
stashing grain and eating their own farm animals before they could
be confiscated. S. J. Taylor noted that "by far the most common
method of resistance had been the peasants' slaughter of their own
livestock in order to prevent collectivization by the State.... In
February and March of 1930 alone some fourteen million head of
cattle were destroyed, one-third of all pigs, one-quarter of all sheep
and goats. During January and February, around ten million peasant households were forced to join the collective farms. By 1934,
the Seventeenth Party Congress announced that more than 40
percent of all cattle in the country had been lost, together with well
in excess of 60 percent of all sheep and goats. Western estimates
were even higher."[11]

Stalin blamed the kulaks and cracked down on them. "The
kulaks were not to be admitted to the collective farms; instead, they
were to be 'liquidated as a class.' This was to take the form of exile

either to Central Asia or to the timber regions of Siberia, where they were used as forced labor in the most dire of circumstances."[12]

The result was a massive famine. Two journalists had the courage to report what was going on. In March 1933, Malcolm Muggeridge wrote in *The Guardian* that people were starving. "I mean starving in the absolute sense; not undernourished as, for instance, most Oriental peasants...and some unemployed workers in Europe, but having had for weeks next to nothing to eat." There was an "all-pervading sight and smell of death." "To say that there is a famine in some of the most fertile parts of Russia is to say much less than the truth; there is not only a famine but—in the case of the North Caucasus at least—a state of war, a military occupation."[13]

A similar eyewitness report by Gareth Jones followed in *The Guardian*. He stayed with peasants who were running out of food. Jones reported that they were "waiting for death" and told him to "Go farther south. There they have nothing. Many houses are empty of people already dead."[14]

Reporters had been barred from traveling to the starving regions, and Soviet officials were furious that these reports by Muggeridge and Jones got out. They threatened to take away reporters' press credentials if these stories were not repudiated. In a *New York Times* article titled "Russians Hungry but not Starving," Duranty took the Soviet line, asserting that "There is no actual starvation or deaths from starvation but there is widespread mortality from diseases due to malnutrition."[15]

Duranty admitted some mismanagement of collective farms and conspiracies by wreckers and spoilers that "made a mess of Soviet food production" but continued that "to put it brutally—you can't make an omelet without breaking eggs, and the Bolshevik leaders are just as indifferent to the casualties that may be involved in their drive toward socialism as any General during the World War who ordered a costly attack."[16]

A few months later, Duranty wrote a colleague that "the 'famine' is mostly bunk" and later that year would go on to write columns with titles like "Soviet Is Winning Faith of Peasants," "Members Enriched in Soviet Commune," and "Abundance Found in North Caucasus."[17]

The reality was quite different. No one knows the precise number of people who died. In his book, *The Harvest of Sorrow: Soviet Collectivization and the Terror-Famine*, Robert Conquest estimates that eleven million people died of starvation in 1932–33 and that seven million of those deaths were in the Ukraine.[18] Most other estimates vary between seven and fourteen million lives lost. This was a predictable consequence of Stalin's policies of agricultural collectivization and forced industrialization.

In a capitalist economy, rising agricultural productivity leads to industrialization. When increases in farm productivity outpace increased demands for food, fewer workers are needed on the farms. Slowly but surely, farm workers find better-paying opportunities in the growing, industrializing cities.

Stalin's economic plan of collectivizing agriculture, exiling Russia's most productive farmers into gulag labor camps, and forcing rural workers into cities to work in state-run industries was a predictable catastrophe. Food production plummeted, and Communist planners gave priority to feeding party members and urban workers, leaving peasants to starve. Communist regimes, from Stalin's to Mao's, have repeatedly followed this disastrous course.[19]

Bob brought up one of the craziest columns in the *New York Times'* Red Century series entitled, "Why Women Had Better Sex

Under Socialism."[20] The author, Kristen Ghodsee, cited a 1990 study finding that East German women had twice the number of orgasms as West German women. Apparently, easygoing socialism lent itself to romance while dog-eat-dog capitalism left women too tired to enjoy a healthy sex life. Or so the argument goes.

Francine du Plessix Gray's book, *Soviet Women: Walking the Tightrope*, paints a rather different picture. Gray interviewed hundreds of Soviet women in the late 1980s. Rather than relaxed women enjoying sex thanks to socialism, as the *New York Times* describes, she found women who were worn out, often from working in physically demanding jobs while still trying to manage their homes and children.

The Bolshevik government declared women's emancipation and employment as one of its goals and passed laws to enforce equal pay for equal work. The reality, Gray found, was quite different. Women earned only about two-thirds of what men did, despite being better educated. Meanwhile, they performed demanding physical labor, the kind usually done by men in market economies. Ninety-eight percent of the janitors and street cleaners in the Soviet Union were women, as well as one-third of railroad workers, and more than two-thirds of highway construction crews and warehouse workers.[21]

Gray noted that while American feminists did not want to be "stuck at home" and were "striving for the right to work in coal mines, firefighting units, police brigades," and other male-dominated occupations, Soviet women were put into these and other arduous jobs, and by the late 1980s, after seventy years of Communism, wanted to be freed from them.[22]

If anything, Soviet women in the 1980s were overworked, and they had a lower standard of living, worse health care, and far more limited options for contraception than women in capitalist countries. A doctor who ran a maternity clinic explained that "unfortunately our condoms are of wretched quality, and the production does not equal the demand...all this contributes to the tragic amounts of deaths we've had from illegal abortions, of which one out of five is fatal."[23]

It's not just that condoms were in short supply. Only 18 percent of women used any method of birth control, and only 5 percent used a modern method, such as the pill or an IUD.[24] As a result, Soviet women had an astounding number of abortions. The Soviet gynecologist Archil Khomassuridze estimated that women in the Soviet Union had between five and eight abortions for each birth.[25]

The Soviet Ministry of Health estimated that there were between two and three abortions for each birth, and even that was five to six times higher than the rate in the United States at the time. But the Ministry of Health statistics only accounted for legal abortions, whereas Khomassuridze was including illegal abortions. His estimates are closer to the United Nations numbers.[26]

Why would women pay bribes for illegal abortions when legal ones were free? Although free, the government-provided ones were gruesome. Olga Lipovskaya, who had two children and seven abortions and was an editor for a feminist magazine, described the process to Gray:

> You go into a hall splattered with blood where two doctors are aborting seven or eight women at the same time; they're usually very rough and rude, shouting at you about keeping your legs wide open et cetera...if you're lucky they give you a little sedative, mostly Valium. Then it's your turn to stagger out to the resting room, where

you're not allowed to spend more than two hours because the production line, you see, is always very busy.[27]

None of this sounds good for women. But what about the better sex part? According to Dr. Khomassuridze, 70 percent of Soviet women had never had an orgasm and "over half of the Soviet women polled outrightly state that they detest sexual contact."[28]

When Gray interviewed Dr. Lev Shcheglov, a sexologist in Leningrad, he explained how cultural factors coupled with the socialist system led to bad sex for women:

> Soviet women may well have the highest rate of culturally repressed orgasm in the world.... Look, what kind of orgasms do you expect in a society which, on top of all the shame we've loaded on sex, lived for decades in communal apartments? I have one couple for whom I've found no solutions; the mother-in-law still sleeps behind a screen in the same room, the young wife can't allow herself to make one moan, one cry.... How, how to make love that way...the mother-in-law lying there hearing every creak of the bedding.[29]

The Soviet socialists promised equality and a better life for women, but just like they failed to deliver on promises of general prosperity and economic equality, it seems that they failed to deliver in the bedroom too.

After downing a few more vodkas, we packed it in for the night so we could get up for our flight the next morning. We flew to Kiev at what Bob called "some stupid-early hour of the morning" to attend the annual meeting of the Economic Freedom Network (EFN), and since he was more awake than I was, I'll let him tell you about Kiev and our follow-on trip to Georgia.

* * *

Thanks, Ben—now maybe we can get some serious economic content into this book. Let me start by saying that the Economic Freedom Network is a regular meeting of academics and policy analysts who work with, and promote, the economic freedom index published in the annual *Economic Freedom of the World* report. This particular meeting attracted about two dozen people from about as many countries to talk about the index and the research that is being done with it.

We were hosted in Kiev by the Bendukidze Free Market Center, a newly formed Ukrainian think tank named after Kakha Bendukidze, a statesman who championed liberal reforms in Georgia. Bendukidze was encouraging similar reforms in the Ukraine at the time of his premature death in 2014.

For twenty-five years I've attended meetings like this, answering questions about the economic freedom index and hearing stories from economists who sometimes face government repression and threats. At this meeting, Jaroslav Romanchuk, an economist from Belarus, mentioned that iPhones are banned from his office, because "You can't take the battery out of an iPhone—and we have to do that so the government can't know our whereabouts." The Ukrainians—none of whom, I noticed, had iPhones—nodded knowingly.

Jaroslav, who served in the Soviet military and is now in his early fifties, is the president of the Scientific Research Mises Center.

In the early 1990s, he participated in a student exchange program and came to the United States. A fellow student gave him a copy of *Atlas Shrugged*. He sent in the card that came with the book to the Ayn Rand Institute, which then sent him ten more books, including *Human Action*, by Ludwig von Mises. That's how Jaroslav learned about free-market economics and classical liberal ideas, which he found not only interesting but convincing.

He half-joked to us that Soviet socialism didn't collapse—it just shrank into Belarus. He might be right. Like North Korea and Cuba, Belarus is one of the few countries where I can't find enough reliable data to rank it in my index. He also told us how poorly women were treated in the Soviet Union, which, for all its vaunted feminism, was a totalitarian state—neither men nor women could escape its repression. Ben asked Jaroslav if he missed anything about the Soviet days. He got a pretty blunt answer: "No. There was nothing good about the Soviet Union. Everything was bad. The army even sent me to Siberia."

Aside from the few breaks in the conference schedule, we had little time for on-the-ground research. After the conference ended, we strolled the streets of Kiev, more in search of a cold beer than more socialism stories, but we couldn't help but comment on how busy people seemed.

Economically speaking, Ukraine is not doing well. It ranks 149th out of 159 countries on the economic freedom index, lower even than Russia (100th). Its estimated average income is $2,100 per person, which is only about 4 percent of the U.S. average. Kiev seemed prosperous, but Kiev is the exception, because Kiev, like Moscow, is a capital city. While the Ukrainian economic reality is probably better than the official figure, there's no question that Ukraine is very poor. The Ukrainian government is corrupt, and it centers a monopolistic economy on benefiting the elites who live in the grand old city of Kiev.

After the fall of the Soviet Union, vast numbers of state-owned assets, ranging from residential buildings to huge industrial factory complexes, needed to be sold off to private owners. The so-called oligarchs, connected friends to the new leadership and old-fashioned mobsters alike, swept in to grab the best assets at rock-bottom prices.

Once the oligarchs got ownership of these state assets, many successfully lobbied to maintain the same monopoly status the firms had enjoyed in Soviet times. State-owned monopolies were replaced with privately owned monopolies. It's understandable that so many Ukrainians felt betrayed after independence.

Kiev seemed prosperous because it is the home of the oligarchs and their minions. We didn't have time to survey the impoverished hinterlands, so we had to be content with surveying central Kiev from fancy bars and restaurants. On our last evening in Kiev, we went to a ridiculously fancy Ukrainian restaurant in an upscale shopping mall in the city center. The mall was next to Independence Square, where demonstrators violently protested the pro-Russian government in 2014. This ultimately led to the installation of the current anti-Russian government. Rows of flowers and pictures of the dead protestors line the square to this day.

Alas, they appear to have died in vain. The new government, while anti-Russian, is arguably as corrupt and authoritarian as the old one, and the local liberals are afraid not only for the country but for themselves personally.

Mikheil Saakashvili (or Misha, as he is called) is the former president of Georgia, and he joined our group for dinner. Since leaving Georgia, he has led the liberal opposition to the current

Ukrainian government. Just before Ben and I arrived in Kiev, the Ukrainian government had revoked Misha's visa, only to return it to him when the incident became a media story. A few weeks after our visit, Saakashvili was accused of colluding with the Russians to undermine the Ukrainian government, arrested, and deported—which was ridiculous, because Misha favors Putin about as much as Ben favors prohibition.

Members of the Economic Freedom Network were joined by former Georgian president Mikheil Saakashvili during a nice meal in Kiev. Saakashvili, who wants to promote liberal reform in Ukraine, was arrested and deported by the authoritarian Ukrainian government shortly after our visit.

But truth doesn't much matter when a socialist government declares you an enemy of the people. When George Orwell wrote his dystopian novel *1984*, it is said that he had the BBC in mind, but he also had Soviet Communism in mind. And for all the "privatization" that has taken place in Russia and Ukraine, both of these countries suffer from a big Communist hangover.

CHAPTER SIX

NEW CAPITALISM: GEORGIA

SEPTEMBER 2017

I f Russia and Ukraine suffer the effects of having imbibed too much Communist vodka, Georgia is like a refreshing sip of Argo beer, one of the country's best brews. I [Bob] love Georgia—the people, the food, the beer, the wine, and of course the economic reforms that have taken a Soviet backwater and given it new life. I've been to Georgia about fifteen times—more than once a year since my first visit in 2005—and consider it almost a second home.

Georgia is bordered by Armenia and Azerbaijan to the south, Turkey to the southwest, and Russia to the north over the Caucasus Mountains. To the east is the Caspian Sea and to the west is the Black Sea, which, through the Bosporus Straits, provides an outlet to the Mediterranean and the larger world. Still, it usually takes me three flights and at least twenty hours to get to Georgia from Texas.

Tbilisi, Georgia's capital, looks nothing like a rich European city. It's shabby and rundown—though a hell of a lot better than it was just a dozen years ago. On my first visit in February 2005, there seemed to be more potholes than cars on the road, and it was cold and dark—not North Korea dark, but close, because the hydroelectric plants could produce only limited energy in the winter. Fuel scarcities meant the gas-powered plants weren't working much either. It was truly dismal.

To be fair, it's been dismal in Georgia for hundreds of years. About the time George Washington was fighting the British with the help of the French, the Georgian King Erekle was fighting the Persians with the help of the Russians. It went better for the Americans. Tbilisi was sacked, and Georgia lost the war. In 1801, Georgia was annexed into the Russian empire. Georgia briefly regained its independence after the Bolshevik Revolution in October 1917, only to have the Red Army invade in 1921.

Bob and Ben pose with Paata Sheshelidze, co-founder of the New Economic School at their headquarters in Tbilisi. Paata and the co-founder of the New Economic School, Gia, were instrumental players in pushing for the reforms that transformed Georgia's economy.

Shortly thereafter, the Georgian Soviet Socialist Republic became a constituent part of the Soviet Union. It wasn't until seventy years later, in April 1991, that Georgia once again became independent of Russia. Even after independence, it remained a pretty dismal place. Civil wars broke out in three regions. Corrupt officials, many of them former Soviets, ran the country into the ground while neglecting to make meaningful, pro-market reforms.

Georgia was still floundering in this state when economists Gia Jandieri and Paata Sheshelidze first brought me to lecture at the New Economic School that they run in Tbilisi. I barely knew Gia and Paata then, and I knew next to nothing about Georgia's history or politics. As we drove through the city, they excitedly pointed out sites where demonstrations had taken place during the Rose Revolution, but I didn't even know what the Rose Revolution was (in case you don't either: it was a peaceful revolution in late 2003 that ousted the corrupt regime that had ruled the country since 1992).

As it turned out, Paata and Gia were instrumental players in the Rose Revolution, and they pushed the new government, led by Mikheil Saakashvili, toward economic freedom. Tall, charismatic, and liberal (in the European sense), Mikheil "Misha" Saakashvili was a stark contrast to the dour ex-Soviet leaders he replaced. He had a law degree from Columbia, spoke impeccable English, wore expensive Italian suits, and gave the Rose Revolution its name by passing out red roses to symbolize his intent to peacefully reform Georgia's institutions. He became the country's new leader in January 2004.

On the first evening of my first trip, Paata and Gia escorted me to a government building where plaster was falling from the walls, wires dangled from the ceiling, and a few bare light bulbs and space heaters were powered by a humming generator. After a terrifying ride in a shaking elevator car with a door that would only close halfway, we arrived to meet the minister of economic reforms, Kakha Bendukidze.

Saakashvili is more of a politician than a policy wonk, and he realized he required help to implement the sort of pro-Western, pro-free-market policies he knew Georgia needed. So he lured biologist-turned-entrepreneur Kakha Bendukidze to be his right-hand man. Bendukidze, a native Georgian, had been running petrochemical companies in Russia and had made a fortune. As the minister of economic reforms, he became the turnaround artist who was able to push through an agenda and jump-start Georgia's economy. Bendukidze was an imposing figure—a hulking beast of a man who must have weighed 350 pounds. I could tell immediately that Kakha was no politician, but I was also excited to learn that he was a fanatical libertarian.

He excitedly rattled off reforms he had initiated and others he had planned. He boasted that he and Saakashvili were "going to make Georgia the freest economy in the world! Freer even than the United States."

Frankly, he sounded insane. But as it turned out, Kakha Bendukidze was crazy like a fox. To list all the reforms Kakha pushed through in those heady days from 2004 to 2006 would require a chapter of its own.[1] He focused on three overlapping goals: reducing the size of the government, privatizing state-owned corporations into independent businesses, and repealing unnecessary bureaucracy, rules, and regulations. Kakha systematically reviewed executive branch jobs; investigated offices in person to see what, if anything, the bureaucrats were doing (the answer in many cases was not much, though they still collected paychecks); and made huge personnel cuts. For instance, he eliminated the superfluous

Department of Pricing (price controls had been lifted more than a decade before), the Price Inspection Office, and the Anti-Monopoly Service, and replaced those three sizeable bureaucracies with a single Agency for Free Trade and Competition, with a staff of six.

In the Ministry of Agriculture, Kakha cut the number of employees from 4,374 to 600; in Tbilisi City Hall, the number of employees fell from 2,500 to 800; the Ministry of Environmental Protection shrank from 5,000 employees to 1,700; and the total number of ministries decreased from 18 to 13. The present Georgian Ministry of Internal Affairs, for example, was formed by merging the Ministry of State Security and the Ministry of Internal Affairs, cutting nearly 50,000 state employees from the public payroll. Kakha also eliminated the utterly corrupt State Traffic Inspection Service that existed merely to extort money from drivers, slashing an estimated 30,000 road police officers from the state payroll and thus, Georgians joked, slashing the crime rate.

Before Kakha's arrival, Georgia's half-hearted efforts at privatization were limited and often corrupt. In 2004, however, Kakha declared that "everything was for sale except Georgia's honor." Most large-scale state properties—factories, hospitals, and residential buildings—were to be privatized in short order.

Under Kakha Bendukidze's initial leadership, Georgia's privatization program was among the most extensive and least corrupt of any former Soviet republic. The government sold off state assets to the highest bidder in public auctions, with no preference given to Georgians over foreigners. There was no corrupt favoritism or insider deals.

The Intourist Hotel, a former gem of a property located in the Black Sea resort town of Batumi, was the very first to be privatized under Bendukidze's new plan. The first potential buyer was a local, would-be crony capitalist with political connections who offered only a paltry $80,000. Bendukidze refused his offer, ignoring political pressures to make the sale, and ordered an open auction. A Russian investor won the auction with a bid of more than $3 million! Kakha dismissed worries that Russians would buy up the country, insisting that private investment was beneficial to Georgia, whatever the source.

Anyone can view recent winning auctions and bid on property online. You can do it right now if you'd like. Check it out at www.privatization.ge. Visa and MasterCard accepted. I checked the site while writing this chapter and noted that a gentleman named Jambul Gelashvili had recently purchased a 50-square-meter (about 538 square foot) concrete building from the state for 2,480 Georgian Lari, or about $975.[2]

Georgia's transparent auctioning of state-owned assets stands in contrast to the privatizations in most other former Communist countries. In most cases, assets were sold at very low prices to political cronies or political leaders themselves. In others, voucher-based privatizations gave citizens coupons with which they could buy stock in newly privatized companies. Unfortunately, many people did not understand the value of the vouchers and were eager to sell them cheaply, even bartering them for food and booze, and unscrupulous brokers took advantage of them.

Private property is essential, but not sufficient, to support a free-market system, which also relies on other economic freedoms—such as the freedom to start a business, produce goods, compete with other businesses, set prices, and hire and fire employees. When Kakha Bendukidze came on the scene, virtually every sphere of the Georgian economy was in desperate need of economic liberalization. Not only did the state own many industries, but taxes were high, and bureaucratic regulation stifled entrepreneurs.

Georgia's post-Soviet income tax and payroll tax systems were designed with the help of the International Monetary Fund and patterned after high-income nations. As a result, the tax system was highly complicated and had steeply progressive tax rates. It was ill suited for Georgia's poor, mostly agricultural economy, and it did little to attract needed foreign investors. In fact, the system was so complex and had so many loopholes that it raised little revenue. Something needed to be done to simplify the tax code, weed out corruption, and generate revenue.

The number of distinct taxes was reduced from twenty-two to seven, and later to six. The rates were also reduced, with a 12 percent flat income tax and a relatively simple 18 percent value-added (or sales) tax. Later, the wage tax, used to fund social pensions, was eliminated and folded into the flat income tax, bringing the total tax rate on wages from 33 percent to 20 percent.

Even as the new reforms took hold, Georgia was still functioning under Soviet-era regulations that gave labor unions special privileges, including mandating that most jobs were reserved for union members. In 2006, that law was finally scrapped, and Georgia adopted a simple, liberalized labor code that opened labor markets to free competition and freedom of contract.

Within a few short years, Kakha had accomplished nearly everything he had promised on that cold February evening in 2005. However, he did fall short of a few goals. His plan to dump the nation's currency in favor of the U.S. dollar, as Panama and Ecuador have done, fell flat. Land privatization efforts in the mountainous parts of Georgia foundered, not so much because of any residual socialist opposition to private property, but because the concept of land ownership is just not very meaningful to the mountain people.

On one trip, I was hiking in the Caucasus Mountains in the northern part of the country, in the region called Khevsureti, which is near the Russian–Chechen border. My Georgian hiking companion and I were staying with a local family far from the nearest road—at least a full day's hike. When our host told me that they don't need private property in the mountains, I politely asked him how he and other hill people kept track of their cows and sheep that grazed along the mountains. With fiery eyes, he replied, "I know my animals!" In other words, like mountain people all over the world, he didn't need any city slickers from the capital interfering in his way of life.

When Kakha began his reforms in 2004, Georgia ranked fifty-sixth on the economic freedom index. In the 2017 edition of the index, Georgia ranked eighth in the entire world, ahead of the eleventh-ranked United States. Can you imagine going from being the Georgian Soviet Socialist Republic in 1991, with almost no economic freedoms, to placing among the freer economies in the world in just a little over a decade? It is truly remarkable.

When Ben visited Georgia with me in the fall of 2017, Tbilisi was no longer a cold, dark city. This was Ben's first experience in Georgia, and he thought it looked and felt pretty rough—and roughest of all was his hotel towel. The hotel still dried them on a clothesline. Ben was convinced his had been starched.

My visits to Tbilisi remind me of watching a favorite niece or nephew—one you see only once or twice a year—grow up. Today's Tbilisi has better-paved streets than Dallas. The once dark city now gleams like Paris at night. Tourists come from all over Europe and the Middle East to enjoy Georgia's famous food, wine, and other attractions, including a new glass pedestrian bridge across the Kura River, the redeveloped medieval section of town with its quaint shops and hip restaurants, the funicular that takes you to a mountaintop where there is a repaired Ferris wheel, and the cable cars that link one mountaintop with another.

Even under Soviet domination, Georgia was far enough from Moscow that it was a center for fine cuisine and avant-garde culture. Tbilisi was a hotbed for filmmakers and artists, like the Tbilisi-born Armenian Sergei Parajanov, who is celebrated today with a whimsical statue of a winged artist soaring through the sky. If the real Parajanov could have soared, he might have avoided the years he spent in Stalin's prisons. The best Soviet chefs were trained in Tbilisi and, to this day, it is common to find Georgian chefs in the kitchens of the finest restaurants throughout the old Soviet Union.

We, of course, took full advantage of the renowned food and drink during this trip. Georgia's wine industry is flourishing, and we were more than happy to sample it. It seems like half the men in Georgia are named Giorgi, and we met one at a restaurant that served his award-winning wines. Giorgi trained as a physicist, as many intelligent people did in the former Soviet Union, because it was easier to maintain one's integrity in the hard sciences like physics and math than in the more overtly politicized fields of history, political science, and economics, all of which had to parrot the Communist Party line. The Soviet Union hopelessly under-produced things like toilet paper and butter, but its education system massively overproduced physicists and mathematicians to the point that some, like Giorgi, ended up making wine.

Actually, even Soviet bureaucrats recognized that Georgia's relatively dry, warm climate was better suited to winemaking than, say, Siberia's, so they designated entire swaths of Georgia's flat central valley east of Tbilisi for winemaking. They imported French grapes and used modern techniques to turn out huge volumes of barely drinkable swill for the masses. Today, no one wants to drink that crap and most of those fields lie fallow, but thankfully the true Georgian wine tradition was kept alive.

Giorgi, for instance, uses native grape varietals that he ferments the Georgian way: crushing the grapes (skins, seeds, stems, and all), pouring the resulting mix into huge clay pots called *qvevri*, burying the pots in the ground, and then waiting for the right moment. The process might sound primitive, but the wines are surprisingly complex, and the white wines especially come out a deep, nearly orange color from interacting with the skins and seeds. Georgian wines are rightly famous and qualify as a tourist attraction on their own, and investors are flocking to get a piece of the action.

Although we enjoyed plenty of good food and drink, we had an aggressive schedule that involved lectures at several local universities. Over the course of three days we each gave lectures at the University of Georgia, International Black Sea University, and the University of Gori on economic freedom, development, and international trade.

Students were always excited to learn that Georgia was among the most economically free countries in the world, but after hearing about how economic freedom creates prosperity, they always had the same question: "If Georgia is so free, why are we so poor?" It's a good question. Other factors besides economic freedom can limit development. Georgia has a difficult geographical location, and its large, hostile neighbor isn't much help either.

And when I say hostile, I really mean it. In August 2008, I was invited by my friends Paata and Gia to lecture at a conference. Just as I hopped on the plane, the Russians invaded Georgia, and when I landed, I found myself in the middle of a war! The Russian army claimed it was assisting the South Ossetians, who wanted autonomy from the Georgian state. The war lasted several days; the Georgians were handily defeated; and to this day two Georgian regions, South Ossetia and Abkhazia, remain under Russian occupation.

The main reason that Georgia is still poor—with incomes that average only about $8,000 per year—is because it was a Russian, and then Soviet, client state for more than two hundred years, spent the first dozen years after the collapse of the Soviet Union pursuing largely socialist policies, and has only recently embraced economic freedom and capitalism. Economic growth compounds over time to raise living standards. Georgia's reform efforts *have* spurred significant growth, so while Georgia can't yet boast of prosperity, it is certainly doing far better than it was, and the future looks much brighter. The evidence was not only visible all around us; it can be seen in the country's measurable economic statistics. Ben's colleagues at Texas Tech, Kevin Grier and Sam Absher, and I have examined the impact of the Rose Revolution on Georgia's social and economic outcomes since 2004.[3] According to our conservative estimates, Georgia's income per person is about 40 percent higher; infant mortality is about 30 percent lower; and employment is about 10 percent higher thanks to the reforms of the Rose Revolution. Moreover, this progress has come without any significant increase in economic inequality. In Georgia, increasing income and opportunity is shared by virtually everyone. The data tell the story, and our eyes confirmed it on this trip.

If Georgia sticks with its reforms, things will keep improving, and some day, Georgian students will not have to ask why their country is poor.

One afternoon in Tbilisi, we went to a converted old factory where, on the ground floor, hipsters drank high-end coffee and munched on gluten-free, vegetarian snacks, while in a conference room on the floor above we participated in a panel discussion about Georgia's "Law on Economic Freedom." That law limits the government to an annual budget deficit of no more than 3 percent of GDP, the national debt to no more than 60 percent of GDP, annual government spending to no more than 30 percent of GDP, and prohibits any new tax without voter approval.

The government that had replaced Saakashvili's wanted to relax these budgetary constraints. Ben and I made the case that as members of a former Communist state, Georgians should know as well as anyone that governments have an insatiable appetite for taxpayer money and a dangerous desire for power over individuals, and that the existing law was a godsend to limit state power, keep reasonable finances, and protect individual freedom. We argued that they should cherish the law rather than dismantle it. A government bureaucrat and a left-wing professor argued against us. After about an hour, we left the Georgians to battle it out in their own language and went in search of beer, which we found in a bar full of bearded hipsters. A week later, we were happy to learn that Georgia's parliament had voted to keep the law intact for another ten years.

After our talks at the University of Gori, we felt obligated to spend an hour or so touring the local Stalin museum. Josef Stalin was born in Gori as Ioseb Jughashvili in 1878. Stalin received a good education at church schools, including seminary studies in Tbilisi, but he was badly behaved and had no intention of becoming a priest. In fact, he had converted to the ideals of atheistic, revolutionary Marxism by the time he left school in 1899. He soon became a protégé of Lenin, eventually adopted the name Stalin, and became a prominent Bolshevik leader and eventually Lenin's successor as head of the Soviet Union and its Communist Party. There was no mention in the museum of any of the atrocities committed by Stalin, except for one small display about Georgian Communists who had been killed on his orders.

We already described the intentional famine Stalin inflicted on the Ukraine, but that's only one of the atrocities Stalin carried out on the citizens of the Soviet Union. During his reign, millions more were executed or worked to death in slave labor camps. According to the most conservative estimates, Stalin is responsible for just shy of ten million deaths, excluding the Ukrainian famine and war-related fatalities. Other estimates are as high as twenty million. Stalin probably ranks just behind Mao as history's second greatest mass murderer, with Hitler coming in third—and all three dictators were, of course, committed socialists of one sort or another.

The locals are oddly proud of Stalin being a native son, and Gori kept a large statue of Stalin near the town hall until 2010, when Saakashvili's government flew an army helicopter to the city in the middle of the night and snatched it away.

Our last stop in Georgia was in the wine country near Telavi, to visit Gia's aunt. Aunt Nino is a bit of a local entrepreneur who runs several businesses in the area, as well as the family's farm. Nino lives in a large home with her very elderly mother, but her husband and two sons have lived and worked in Brooklyn for several years. The remittances they send home help explain the new modern kitchen and fireplace on the ground floor. While we skewered and barbecued the pork that was butchered only that morning, the women busily prepared a myriad of side dishes. We were in for a mini *supra*!

The supra, a Georgian feast, is one of the most elaborate meals one can experience. The eating and drinking can begin before sundown and go until sunrise. This was Ben's first time in a regular Georgian home, and he didn't understand my excitement. The women began to bring out *khinkali*, my favorite dumplings in the world; *khachapuri*, the best cheesy bread ever made; *badrijani*, delicious eggplant and walnut rolls; *shashlik*, skewered meats; *sulguni*, fresh cow cheese; and on and on, until the small table was heaping with food. Oh, let's not forget the homemade wine, gallons and gallons of fresh, semi-sweet, peachy-colored wine in two-liter bottles that lined the kitchen table. After a small plate or two, the inevitable toasting began.

Gia, as the senior male in the household, became the *tamada*, the toastmaster. At any proper supra, the tamada initiates each round of toasts, starting usually with a toast to family members, then to ancestors, then to the Holy Trinity, and then to whatever comes up. He drinks after his toast, and then the next person is expected to individually offer a toast closely related to the tamada's toast and drink, and then the next person goes, and so on. After everyone is done with that round, the tamada begins anew.

After several rounds, Gia initiated a toast to lost friends. But Ben was still unclear on the rules and tried to toast to free markets or something, and we all screamed, "No! You can't toast to that now!" He was utterly baffled, and I don't think ever completely caught on to the game.

Gia Jandieri, co-founder of the New Economic School, proposes a Georgian toast at an impromptu supra with Bob, Gia's Aunt Nino, her mother, and Ben.

When it was my turn, I toasted Kakha Bendukidze. Kakha's exuberance for economic freedom was matched only by his love of food and drink. A lifetime of excesses led to his death in London in 2014 during a heart operation. By the time of his death, he and Saakashvili had moved to Ukraine to try to kick-start free-market economic reforms there. I still mourn his loss, not only as a champion for freedom, but also as someone who became my friend during my many visits to his country.

Kakha Bendukidze's name and legacy live on, however, in the form of the Bendukidze Free Market Center in Kiev. We can only hope that the center that carries his name will bring Ukraine the same level of economic freedom and ultimate prosperity that his reforms are bringing to Georgia.

CHAPTER SEVEN

CONCLUSION: BACK IN THE USSA

JULY 2018

"W hat's up, Comrade?" I greeted Bob at the conference-level foyer in the Chicago Hyatt Regency, where we had infiltrated the largest annual gathering of American socialists.

"It's like a Bizarro-World version of APEE," he answered.

Had to laugh at that. The Association of Private Enterprise Education (APEE) brings together "teachers and scholars from colleges and universities, public policy institutes, and industry with a common interest in studying and supporting the system of private enterprise."[1] Bob and I are longtime members and past presidents of the association and have served for years on APEE's board of directors. This was definitely not our usual crowd.

We expected—and noticed immediately—the poorly groomed, unhygienic men and the deliberately unattractive women who wanted to strike a blow against the patriarchy. But these folks were actually in the minority. Most of the people in attendance were dressed more casually than you might expect at a conference, but they looked fairly normal.

Our standard economist uniform of khakis, dress shirt, tie, and blue sport coat would have stood out, so we went casual too. My jeans and Brooks Brothers button-down didn't draw any attention. Bob and his colleague Daniel Serralde blended in even better in their Communist-red T-shirts. This was field research. We didn't want to draw unnecessary attention to ourselves, but we weren't there to deceive anyone either.

After traveling the unfree world and witnessing the economic stagnation, starvation, poverty, and political tyranny imposed by socialist regimes, Bob and I came to the Socialism Conference to answer our own question: How can so many Americans, particularly millennials, view socialism so favorably? We wanted to hear what these self-described young socialists had to say, and there were plenty of millennials to ask.

In fact, it was our age more than our attire that made us stand out. Eyeballing the crowd, we guessed that more than two-thirds of the attendees were under thirty-five years old. The next-largest demographic was 1960s-era hippies who were now seventy or older. There were very few people like us, who came of age during the 1980s and '90s, the years of Ronald Reagan, Margaret Thatcher, their successors George H. W. Bush and John Major, and the fall of the Berlin Wall, after which socialism seemed pretty thoroughly refuted.

All down the hallway, young people were selling T-shirts and other merchandise sporting such asinine slogans as "Solidarity," "People over Profit," and "Tax the Rich, A Lot." There was an occasional "Smash Fascism" or "No More Cops" shirt that we could sympathize with, but for the most part it was crazy stuff like Communist cat calendars, which looked like they'd been printed on someone's fifteen-year-old inkjet printer. They were selling for the very capitalistic price of twenty dollars. I nudged Bob with my elbow. "These kids sure seem enterprising for a bunch of commies."

"Nah, this is just a typical socialist black market," he said.

And he was right. It appeared that none of this black-market capitalism was sanctioned. They weren't selling goods from tables that they had registered and paid for with the hotel and conference organizers. They were selling goods willy-nilly, pulling them from duffle bags, stacks on the floor, and cardboard boxes. For whatever reason, normal hotel conference rules weren't being enforced.

Another thing that seemed to be missing was a clear definition of what constituted socialism. Communists and socialists of all stripes agree on at least one thing—that private property should be abolished and replaced with collective ownership. This means that, in practice, the government should control everything that goes into "the means of production," including raw materials, factories, and labor. The government, not individuals, decides what to produce, how to produce, and for whom to produce. But that wasn't the focus of the conference's opening rally.

The rally had three scheduled speakers: activists Haley Pessin and Denise Romero, and Dave Zirin, a sportswriter for the lefty magazine *The Nation*. But everyone got into the act when at one point early in the rally, most of the people in the room started a spontaneous, "Free abortion on demand. We can do it. Yes, we can," chant that lasted a good minute or two.

Although socialist countries like Soviet Russia and Castro's Cuba have high abortion rates, free abortion seemed like an odd item to draw such enthusiasm from people attending the opening rally at a socialist conference. After all, abortion is not exactly a central pillar of a socialist system.

The crowd at the Socialism Conference applauds after a round of cheers for "Free abortion! Yes, we can!"

Oddly, none of the speakers at the opening rally commented on the importance of central planning and abolishing private property. Instead, we heard things like "Damn the Supreme Court to Hell," in reference to the court's recent ruling limiting the power of public unions to coerce fees out of non–union member employees. There was also plenty said about the immigration crisis and the separation of illegal immigrant parents from their children. We were reminded that, "Democrats are deporters too." Of course, President Trump was the frequent target of negative remarks. No big surprise there.

Most of what we heard was just support for a wide array of leftist political positions that have little to do with Marx or socialism. As libertarians, we actually agreed with quite a bit of it, but one thing the attendees didn't seem to know anything about was economics.

Speakers criticized "capitalism"—which they equated with the mixed economy of the United States—but did not talk much about what a socialist system would look like or how it would function. They were passionate about making a world where "people are put before profit," but they did not make a case for how socialism would do this. We heard about the "sick barbaric system called capitalism" and were assured that "Communism will win!" That comment drew an enthusiastic round of applause.

After the rally, Bob and I decided to divide and conquer. He went off to a session about Salvador Allende, the elected socialist leader of Chile who killed himself during a right-wing coup in 1973. After a few minutes, he snuck into my session and sat next to me. "The Allende session was postponed. Apparently, the speaker got called into work," he whispered, barely containing his laughter. I couldn't help but wonder where the speaker was employed.

I attended a session on Korea, curious to hear if that was an example of Communism winning. No such luck. The session, titled "Empire and Resistance: Korea's Secret History," featured lectures by Diana Macasa and David Whitehouse. Diana is a member of the San Francisco branch of the International Socialist Organiza-tion (ISO). David is also a Bay Area activist and has written for a few socialist publications. Diana and David focused most of their remarks on how Korea has struggled against domination by the Japanese, Russian, American, and Chinese imperialists.

Most of what we heard seemed factually accurate, but they failed to discuss the difference between North and South Korea's economic systems. Diana mistakenly claimed that "South Korea today is among the most unequal countries in the world" as a result of capitalism.

But it's not.

Economists use something called a Gini coefficient to measure income inequality across countries. In 2015, South Korea's Gini coefficient of 33.5 ranked it the fifth most equal country out of the eighty-two countries in the world with reported data.[2] More generally, research with Bob's index has shown that there is really no relationship between how capitalist a country is and how unequal its incomes are. The big difference between the poor in freer economies and unfree economies is their average income *level*. In the most economically free countries, the poorest 10 percent of the population earns about $12,000 per year, while the poorest 10 percent of the population in the least free countries earns only $1,100.[3]

In David's part of the talk, he described how the economies of North and South Korea began to diverge in the 1970s. He accurately stated that as many as two million people, or 10 percent of the population in the North, died of starvation in the 1990s. He acknowledged that while the South is unequal, it's relatively rich, and many people must live on less than two dollars a day in the North.

We found it amazing that there was no mention of the fact that North Korea has a socialist economic system and the state owns most of the means of production, while the South has embraced capitalism. Instead, David blamed the North's economic collapse on natural disasters, the end of Soviet aid after the fall of the Soviet Union, and American economic sanctions. But while it's true that Soviet economic aid propped up North Korea, and that freer trade with the United States would benefit the North (and Cuba too, for that matter), Soviet economic aid was never a major cause of economic growth. Most of the capitalist Asian Tiger nations received minimal foreign aid but grew wealthy at precisely the time that North Korea stagnated.

North Korea's state-run economic system is far and away the biggest cause of that country's poverty. Without strong markets, trade with the United States would be like duct tape on a broken car radiator. Blaming natural disasters only invites questions about why natural disasters seem to hit socialist nations so much harder than they hit capitalist nations.

Why were we surprised that the speakers at the Socialism Conference didn't talk much about socialism? Well, I guess no one wants to admit that they like a system like North Korea's. Still, the International Socialist Organization, which has branches in about forty U.S. cities, was one of the sponsors of the conference, and many of its members were in attendance. The ISO is pretty explicit that it wants true socialism—that is, socialism the way Bob and I are using the term. The ISO's website has a manifesto titled "Where We Stand." Its opening paragraph reads:

> War, poverty, exploitation and oppression are products of the capitalist system, a system in which a minority ruling class profits from the labor of the majority. The alternative is socialism, a society based on workers collectively owning and controlling the wealth their labor creates. We stand in the Marxist tradition, founded by Karl Marx and Frederick Engels, and continued by V.I. Lenin, Rosa Luxemburg and Leon Trotsky.[4]

Notably absent from that list of names are Kim Il-Sung, Castro, Mao, and Stalin. You see, "A socialist society can only be built when workers collectively take control of that wealth and *demo-cratically* plan its production and distribution according to human needs instead of profit" (emphasis added).[5] Inserting the magic word "democratic" allows them to claim that "China and Cuba, like the former Soviet Union and Eastern Bloc, have nothing to do with socialism. They are state capitalist regimes. We support the struggles of workers in these countries against the bureaucratic ruling class."[6]

In short, the ISO supports the essential defining feature of socialism—abolishing the private ownership of the means of production and replacing it with collective ownership, which in turn means replacing markets with central planning. But then by inserting "democratic" into planning, it gets to claim that real-world implementations of collective ownership, which has always resulted in political tyranny, isn't what they mean. Oh, but wait, remember Venezuela? That was democratic socialism, right? Wrong. Bob will have to explain. I missed that session.

* * *

It was day two. Wearing my Cincinnati Reds cap (ha ha, get it?), I was in a room packed with young socialists waiting for the session called "Did Socialism Fail in Venezuela?" I expected to hear either an admission that the Venezuelan socialist economic model had failed (but for reasons aside from socialism, such as falling oil prices) or an optimistic assertion that it was still succeeding, despite all the current evidence to the contrary, and that time would prove the socialists right.

The speaker, Eva Maria, was a Venezuelan-born socialist who now lives in Portland. Eva gave a very sophisticated and mostly first-rate rundown of the current crisis in Venezuela. She talked about food shortages, corruption, and Maduro's political crackdown with a degree of honesty that I admit surprised me. She even acknowledged that most of the social gains in Venezuela were because of high oil prices in the mid-2000s that filled the state's coffers and allowed it to spend more on health care and education.

After about thirty minutes, she switched gears and began to denounce the "state capitalist" system of Chavez and Maduro in Venezuela.

Wait? What? Did she say the capitalist system of Venezuela?

Yep, she did. "Socialism has not failed in Venezuela, because it has never been tried!" she shouted to wild applause in the steamy and increasingly odorous room.

If option one was admitting that Venezuelan socialism had failed, and option two was maintaining that it would still be vindicated, I was certainly not expecting option three, which was arguing that Venezuela's economy had collapsed because it was too capitalistic! Notwithstanding the socialist rhetoric of Chavez and Maduro, and despite the praise they had received from Western socialists, Venezuela is really just as capitalist as the good ol' U.S. of A.

Or so she claimed.

I must have missed class that day in graduate school when the professor explained that nationalizing firms and controlling prices were hallmarks of capitalism.

This is the same dirty trick socialists have played for decades. Whenever things go south, as they inevitably do, they claim that it wasn't "real" socialism. I find the whole thing more than a little disingenuous and very irritating. When socialists, democratic and otherwise, held up Venezuela as a great socialist experiment in the

2000s, the message was, "See, we told you so; socialism works!" But when the failure happened, the message changed to, "No, wait—that's not real socialism!" They want to claim socialism during the good times but disavow it during the bad.

Perhaps I shouldn't be too harsh here. I am sure many of the people in attendance at this conference were not extolling Venezuela's kind of socialism even in the heady days of the 2000s, when Sean Penn and others were singing its praises. The socialists at this conference seemed to prefer something called "socialism from below," an idealized world in which workers communally own firms and trade only locally with other worker-run firms. It's almost anarchic, as there's little role for the state. I have to grant that this utopian, stateless vision is not what has been tried in the USSR, China, Cuba, or Venezuela.

Still, I'm not sure how this ideology jibes with the practice of real-world socialism. Lenin and Trotsky were not leaders of a hippie commune—they literally created state socialism and tried to spread it around the world. To separate the state from socialism in any large society is like trying to separate private property from capitalism. It can't be done. I'll say it once more for the people in the back: socialism, in practice, means that *the state owns and controls the means of production*. This is what socialism meant to Lenin and Trotsky, and this is what socialism means today.

If these kids want to live on communes and call it socialism, then Ben and I encourage them to do so. They should understand, though, that small voluntary communes suffer from the same economic information and incentive problems that larger socialist systems do, just on a smaller scale. Invariably, they have to rely on markets outside the commune because the division of labor, among such a small population, will be unable to supply all of the community's wants (unless they're willing to accept a very low standard of living).[7] Your commune ain't gonna make an iPhone, comrade.

The young, naïve socialists who dream of socialism "from below" are caught in a conundrum. Non-state socialist communes can only work (poorly) on a small scale in an otherwise capitalist world. To replace capitalism with this system necessitates centralizing power in order to plan the economy. That ultimately results in state ownership, control, and tyranny. Society-wide socialism "from below" that doesn't entail state ownership is a contradiction in terms.

* * *

So what the hell is socialism if every country that has ever collectivized the means of production is not socialist? Many of the conference attendees we asked thought socialism meant simply aspiring toward a world with better conditions for various marginalized groups. Few correctly identified collectivism or state ownership of the means of production as the defining characteristic of socialism, and most had not come here to celebrate that.

I [Ben] spoke with three young women after the conclusion of the opening rally, all of whom were associated with the Berkeley International Socialist Organization. I told them I was writing a book on socialism and asked if they'd mind answering some questions so that I could better understand what attracts younger people to socialism. They readily agreed. I asked them why they attended the conference.

An attractive, well-dressed woman answered first. "The urgency is because of Trump, immigrant rights, Black Lives Matter, indigenous rights."

Her friend said she "wanted to meet a lot of comrades."

The third woman had a streak of green dyed into her hair and unshaved legs. She told me she was "new to socialism, and here to learn with my best friend, but also for the solidarity of it all."

I asked them to describe the essence of socialism. One answered that "uncompromising socialism is fully committed to systematic change and ending oppression of all types." I asked if that meant abolishing private property and was told, "Abolish everything—not just private property. Abolish borders, rent, everything." She also said some shit about intersectionality that I didn't understand.

By this point in the book, I bet you're not surprised that Bob and I hit the hotel bar after the last evening session. The objective was to continue interviewing the conference attendees, of course. Anti-Hero IPA was on tap. The handle was a green raised fist with a bright red star on the wrist.

Anti-Hero IPA is a product of Revolution Brewing, Illinois's largest independently owned brewing company. The hotel obviously knew its audience this weekend. It sold well, and it tasted good too. It's one of the twenty-seven different major beers made by Revolution Brewing, which also makes scores of other specialty brews. In addition to IPAs, the company brews Belgian quadrupels, barley wines, American-style lagers, oatmeal stouts, reds, and many other varieties. Alcohol contents range from 2.3 percent in a grapefruit radler to 16.6 percent in a barley wine. Many of the company's cans and tap handles feature raised fists, red stars, and other Marxist-inspired images.

But let me tell you—this privately owned company produces a variety and quality of beer that no socialist country we visited could touch. And the kids were drinking it up. Though, in fairness, I bet they would have drunk the bland Cuban beer and perhaps the god-awful North Korean beer if they had been on tap too.

That evening, we each had conversations similar to the one I'd had earlier with the young women from Berkeley. Bob went outside and bummed a cigarette from a young man who appeared to be carrying all his worldly possessions in his backpack. Bob asked how he got interested in socialism. His answer, and I swear this is true, was that he saw a Che T-shirt at a bar one night and decided to research Che and the Cuban Revolution. Make fun of the propaganda T-shirts all you want, but they recruit new comrades to the cause.

Our friend Daniel Serralde actually comes from a socialist family. When a young lady at the bar overheard this she practically gushed, "Oh my gawd, are you a red diaper baby?!" He said, "Almost." Daniel explained that his grandfather was Basque and Jewish and fought with the Republicans against Franco. "COOL!" she practically squealed. Having a relative who fought against the fascists gives you some serious street cred with this crowd.

Bob talked to two young women who had progressed from pro-choice activism to full-blown socialist activism; and, indeed, abortion and environmental activism seem to be common gateway drugs to socialism. Many of the conference sessions reflected a broad concern for "social justice" issues; abolishing private property and replacing it with collective ownership was more of an afterthought.

If you want to get a flavor of what really interested the attendees at the conference, aside from singing the praises of Marx and Lenin, here's a list of some of the conference sessions:

- Black Lives Matter at School

- A World Without Borders? Marxism, Nations, and Migration
- Capitalism and the Gender Binary
- The Rise of Red Power and the American Indian Movement
- Artists Against War
- Gender and Disability
- Whose Clinics? Our Clinics! Defending Abortion rights
- What Do Socialists Say About White Privilege?
- All Eleven Million: The Fight for Immigrant Rights
- From TrumpCare to Medicare for All: The Growing Movement for Single-Payer Health Care
- Socialism and Women's Liberation
- Athletes in Revolt: Black Lives Matter in Sports Today
- U.S. Imperialism under Trump
- From #MeToo to No More: How Can We End Sexual Harassment and Assault?
- CSI Is Lying to You: Junk Science in Criminal Convictions
- Queens of the Resistance: A Revolutionary Drag Show

The thing is, Bob and I are also concerned with a lot of the same issues discussed in these sessions, but it's not obvious what they have to do with socialism. I went to the "World Without Borders" session. The speaker was Denise Romero, one of the activists from the opening rally. She said a lot of things that were certifiably crazy. For instance, she claimed, "Capitalism is failing because it overproduces things and then can't sell it."

Um, no.

People have a virtually limitless desire for goods and services in general, but if any particular good or service is overproduced, the price falls and companies adjust their production downward.

Another doozy was her statement that "the North American Free Trade Agreement [NAFTA] is bad because it's exploiting Mexicans." Actually, NAFTA has promoted Mexican economic growth and lifted many people out of poverty. This strong Mexican economic growth has actually stemmed the tide of migration. While migration from Mexico surged in the early days of NAFTA, more recently, more Mexicans have returned home than have come to the United States.[8]

Neither Bob nor I like borders, or what he calls "lines politicians draw on maps." We're both big free trade advocates. Since the time of Adam Smith, economists have understood that when goods are traded between countries, it makes people on both sides of the border richer. Ditto for free capital flows. And guess what, the same is true for people who want to move. We think people should be free to move between countries, because it benefits both the migrants and the native-born citizens in the destination countries.

Does that last part surprise you? It shouldn't. Capitalism, by which we mean free markets, eschews any government rules or regulations that prohibit responsible adults, regardless of where they happen to live, from making trades.

When a worker moves from Massachusetts or Ohio to work in Texas, as Bob and I did, he does so because he thinks it's in his self-interest, and the employer who hires him obviously thinks he's the best candidate available. The economics underlying our choices are no different whether the worker is a Mexican or a Somali or an Indonesian.

Economists estimate that if international immigration restrictions were removed, we'd have massive global economic gains. Economist Michael Clemens has suggested that the gains would range from 50 to 150 percent of *world* GDP.[9] On average, that's a doubling of global income. The largest gainers would be the immigrants themselves. Greater global migration would contribute to a massive reduction in world poverty—just as internal migration has in China today, as we saw in Beijing and Shanghai.

This may come as a surprise to people who watch Fox News, but native-born citizens in destination countries win too. On average, incomes go up for natives when immigrants move in. Of course, some immigrants take jobs from some of the native-born citizens, but immigration also creates other jobs at the same time, because immigrants demand goods and services too. Immigration, like international trade in goods, both creates and destroys jobs. The long-run net effect on the total number of jobs for natives, though, is a wash. International trade, whether in labor (through migration) or in goods (through imports and exports), changes the mix of jobs and makes us all more productive.

Virtually all of the conservative fears related to immigration—how it affects our economy, jobs, wages, and the welfare state—are out of step with the social-science research done by economists. I edited a whole book on the topic. Like this book, it's written for normal people to understand, but without all the fun drinking and carousing.[10]

Most immigration is caused by oppressive government policies in origin countries. Migrants move from poorer, less free countries to richer, more economically free countries.

There's a reason the boats don't sail from Miami to Havana.

In fact, it's no accident that socialist countries build walls, guard towers, and minefields to keep their citizens in. Denise Romero forgot to mention this in her "World Without Borders" talk at the socialist conference. But we agree with Denise that some migration was forced by bad U.S. policy. She pointed out, "Ending the war on drugs and war on terror will result in fewer people needing to migrate." We agree. The U.S. government's war on drugs is unwinnable because, in the language of economists, it is a supply-side war, where demand isn't very price-sensitive.

That means when the U.S. government scores a "win" in the war, the price of the remaining drugs goes up more than the usage falls. As a result, net revenue to drug cartels increases, which increases their ability to corrupt law enforcement and buy weapons and other smuggling equipment. The result has been an endless cycle of increasing violence along the entire supply chain in Central and South America, and it has surely resulted in some people emigrating out of the most violent areas.

We feel the same about the war on terror. The wars and violence associated with it in the Middle East are a major reason for Europe's immigration wave. However, our reservations about the war on terror and U.S. militarism overseas are broader than just their effect on immigration. Thus, we sympathized with the points made in conference sessions "Artists Against War" (though we're not at all artsy) and "U.S. Imperialism under Trump." But being against war doesn't require being anti-capitalism and pro-socialism. It requires being against, well, war.

In fact, advocates for capitalism can be against war precisely because war undermines capitalist institutions and freedoms. Our economist friend, Chris Coyne, wrote a book entitled *After War: The Political Economy of Exporting Democracy*, in which he shows that when the U.S. engages in foreign intervention, it rarely creates the kind of lasting institutional change that supports what some might call a "neoliberal" society.[11]

Economist Robert Higgs's classic book, *Crisis and Leviathan*, shows how crises in the United States, especially wars, have led to expanded government at the expense of markets.[12] Chris's latest book, *Tyranny Comes Home: The Domestic Fate of U.S. Militarism*, co-authored with another friend of ours, Abby Hall, has shown how U.S. military interventions abroad "boomerang" back to the United States in ways that decrease our freedoms at home.[13] See, anti-war isn't a uniquely leftist position. Capitalists should be anti-war too. We're anti-war, anti–border walls, and pro–free trade (which includes freedom of movement).

Pro-market guys like us have reservations about the criminal justice system too. The conference organizers should have invited our non-socialist buddy Roger Koppl to give a talk during their session "CSI is Lying to You: Junk Science in Criminal Convictions." Roger's book *Expert Failure* is among the best on the topic.[14]

We could go on, but we think you get the idea. The United States has plenty of problems. Agreeing that something is a problem doesn't mean that socialism is the solution. In fact, we think most of the problems identified by socialists, especially poverty and inequality, are a result of too much government—not too little. Although the United States organizes the bulk of its economic activity through markets (remember, it ranks eleventh on Bob's economic freedom index), it is far from the free-market, capitalist society Bob and I favor. We think eliminating many existing government interventions and allowing a greater reliance on markets and voluntary civil society is the best way to address all the major problems our country has.

The socialist conference we attended in Chicago was not at all unusual. In fact, it was consistent with the wider socialist network in its focus not on socialism per se (or as it really is), but on leftist-liberalism generally. The July/August 2018 issue of *Washington Monthly* did an in-depth story titled "The Socialist Network: Are today's young, Bernie-inspired leftist intellectuals really just New Deal liberals?" that examines whether the beliefs of prominent young socialists are actually consistent with the definition of socialism.[15]

In a speech at Georgetown University in the fall of 2015, self-proclaimed socialist Bernie Sanders stated, "I don't believe the government should own the corner drugstore or the means of production, but I do believe that the middle class and working families who produce the wealth of America deserve a fair deal." Um, hello? Not socialism. You're spotting it, too, aren't you?

Nathan Robinson, editor of *Current Affairs*, wrote that either "(1) Bernie Sanders is unaware of the definition of socialism, or (2) Bernie Sanders is fully aware of the definition of socialism, and is lying about it," and "Socialism means an end to capitalism. Bernie Sanders does not want to end capitalism. Bernie Sanders is not a socialist."

But in his interview with *Washington Monthly,* Nathan Robinson admitted, "I've sort of come around to the idea that 'socialism,' the word, should less be used to describe a state-owned or collectively owned economy, and more used to describe a very strong commitment to a certain fundamental set of principles. It should be used to describe the position that is horrified by solvable economic depravations, rather than a very specific and narrow way of ordering the economic system."

Meanwhile, in the very magazine Robinson edits, Fredrik deBoer said that socialists "seem to be falling into the models of the welfare state without really knowing we're doing it." As summarized by *Washington Monthly*, deBoer argued that "socialism means moving sectors of the economy into communal ownership—not merely expanding the welfare state, which is social democracy."

We saw this same range of conflicting opinions at the conference, too. On my last night there, I asked a young man in the bar about the Hartford Whalers hat he was wearing. He was from one of the New England branches of the International Socialist Organization. Remember, that's the group that wants democratic socialism with collective ownership.

I asked him if most people at the conference were really socialist—that is, did they believe in abolishing private property and insisting on state ownership of the means of production. He answered that, "You don't become a radical overnight. They have to start somewhere."

He himself claimed to identify as a real radical who wanted real socialism. So, I asked him to pick a country closest to his ideal system. He told me all countries are so far away from what he wants that it's hard to say, but, if forced to pick, "I guess a Nordic country with a big welfare state."

Okay, so let's return to the question we started with. Why is socialism popular with millennials? We think a significant number of them identify as socialists without understanding socialism's defining characteristic—which is state ownership of the means of production and the abolishment of private property.

They define socialism as a more radical brand of progressive or leftist beliefs.

A significant number of socialist leaders at this conference, however, *did* support socialism as we understand the term and would socialize the means of production if given the chance. We fear that they are using social justice causes like abortion, the environment, and immigrant rights to bring more young people into the fold.

This is about more than semantics.

Socialist leaders see that they have an opportunity with young people if they identify socialism as an ideology that is pro-abortion and pro-environment. (It has certainly been the former, in practice, though not the latter, and neither issue is central to socialism.) But if they convince young people that "social justice" equals socialism, that true pro-choice, pro-immigrant, pro-environment activists should be socialists and repudiate private property and embrace collectivization or state ownership of the means of production, it's likely that a good many of them will.

This is a slippery slope, and it's not a new strategy.

Most peasants who supported the Bolshevik Revolution didn't know or care about Karl Marx; they just wanted freedom from the tsar. They didn't know that the Bolsheviks would later collectivize their farms, immiserate them, starve them, and exile them to Siberia.

The typical comrade attending the socialist conference in Chicago wasn't an evil jerk who wanted to see more suffering and tyranny. The typical comrade there only wanted "socialism from below" or "democratic socialism" or leftist-liberalism to the max.

But they fail to see two important things. First, whether you call it democratic or not, collective ownership fails to create the powerful incentives and market information that are necessary to create economic prosperity. It is a demonstrable fact that socialist systems inevitably lead to economic stagnation and leave average people much worse off than they would be under a capitalist system.

Second, collective ownership, and the centralization of power that comes with it, is an invitation to tyranny that has been accepted by socialist regimes over and over again, almost without fail.

In the end, we're inclined to agree with a point made by Liz Bruenig, the young columnist for the *Washington Post*, who caused a stir recently with her article titled, "It's Time to Give Socialism a Try."[16] After receiving a lot of negative responses, she wrote in a follow-up column, "It makes sense to think of socialism on a spectrum, with countries and poles being more or less socialist, rather than either/or."[17] We're sympathetic to this point. Full socialism (no markets) and full capitalism (all markets) are opposite poles on a spectrum. Every country on earth is somewhere in between. In fact, Bob's spent most of his career creating and updating an index that basically measures where on the socialism-to-capitalism spectrum different countries fall.

Both economic theory and empirical evidence suggest that countries that embrace markets to a greater extent and eschew socialist policies to a greater extent enable humans to live wealthier, longer, better, and more fulfilling lives. And after trotting around the globe to visit many of the countries that are on or have been on the spectrum nearest to pure socialism, we can confidently attest that socialism just plain sucks.

AFTER-DINNER DRINKS WITH MATT KIBBE

A t least a dozen beer cans covered the top of the table in the BlazeTV studio when we sat down to talk with Matt Kibbe. Some were fancy IPAs and Pale Ales that Matt likes, but there was also Venezuelan and North Korean swill. Matt had a simple plan for our interview on his show: he wanted us to do the economic equivalent of a *Drunk History* video. But first, we had a different type of experiment for him.

We decided to "live write" a postscript for this book by interviewing Matt. The three of us share broadly similar economic, philosophical, and historical views when it comes to capitalism and socialism. But Matt's not an egghead academic like us. He's a freedom fighter who has fought the grassroots political battles in the trenches.

Matt's currently the president and chief community organizer at Free the People. Before that he was the founder and president of FreedomWorks for many years. Under Matt's leadership, FreedomWorks played an important role in sparking and organizing the Tea Party movement a decade ago. FreedomWorks was the lead organizer of the Taxpayer March on Washington in 2009.

This puts Matt in a different position than Bob and me to provide insight into the grassroots socialist movement energizing young people today. A decade ago, it was a youth for Ron Paul movement that he folded into the Tea Party. What's changed with young people today?

Much like the rest of this book, we did this interview by the seat of our pants, while consuming a fair bit of beer. So, we've edited the transcript to make it a bit more readable.

Powell: Matt, take us back to the 2008 presidential campaign and Ron Paul in the primaries, and the big push that young people gave for what the mainstream commentators and Republican Party would call "a crazy old man" who articulated liberty. What was it with him and his movement that young people identified with that gave him the legs to get to the national stage, and really launch what became the Tea Party movement afterwards?

Kibbe: Two things. First of all, it was his authenticity. You can sort of struggle with this because Ron Paul is not a typical movie-star-looking kinda guy. He's not necessarily someone that can always tell the most articulate story. But he's the real deal. He's been talking about ending the Federal Reserve and getting out of our endless wars since day one. So that was part of it, I think. That was part of his sales pitch. He's authentic, he's talking about principles.

The other part is technology. The Ron Paul money bombs online were some of the first demonstrable, measurable, primal screams from the grassroots—an early indicator that the establishment was about to be challenged by insurgent outsider candidates who had a different perspective. He was not from your mother's Republican Party. He was something else. And so there was this process by which technology decentralized politics a little bit and empowered disenfranchised voters. The Tea Party took that and ran with it, and created a sustained social movement... bigger perhaps, and not so dependent on a personality like Ron Paul.

But, fast-forward to today and you could say the same thing about Bernie Sanders, you could say the same thing about Alexandria Ocasio-Cortez, and even Donald Trump in a different way. He is sort of a pop-star character from his television shows. All of these candidates use technology. All of them, in their own way, are sort of authentic.

Powell: So, before we jump so far ahead to the socialists and what's resonating now, what happened to the movement that became the Tea Party? It was this grassroots movement that was decentralized, and it challenged the mainstream Republican Party and elected a wave of candidates in 2010. Where has it gone?

Kibbe: So those people are still there. And I still view the Tea Party—as someone who was fully involved in it—as one of the most influential social movements in my lifetime, second only to the civil rights movement. They had core values. You could wander into any Tea Party crowd in 2009 and 2010 and virtually any individual activist would tell you: "I'm for individual liberty, fiscal responsibility, and constitutionally limited government." They would all say the same thing and those values held it together. That's what made it such a potent social movement.

Then opportunistic politicians jumped up on stage, and that ultimately broke the party up. You fill the National Mall in Washington, D.C., with people representing potential votes, and politicians are going to be attracted, sort of like flies to... flypaper. You thought I was going to say something else, right? So yeah, like flies to shit. All of a sudden, the community moved away from those principles and started thinking about political wins. Politics divides people, and Donald Trump's candidacy succeeded in breaking up the once mighty Tea Party once and for all. But you know, politics happens at the margin, and small margins lead to big differences in outcomes. Those liberty-minded activists, at least the ones from the Ron Paul movement and the libertarians and the constitutional conservatives, they are still there, but they no longer represent a cohesive social movement that will impact political decisions in the same way they did in 2010.

Lawson: Could you draw some similarities to the socialist movement around Bernie and AOC today to what you saw watching the Ron Paul movement? Also, maybe you could prognosticate, how is it going to turn out for this social movement? Is this socialist movement going to work out better or worse for them than the Tea Party movement did for its participants?

Kibbe: Some of my Ron Paul friends get upset about this, but I often compare Bernie Sanders to Ron Paul, because they have a similar persona. The one thing about their authenticity is they've been talking about the same stuff from day one. Ron Paul was always this cranky antiwar libertarian and Bernie Sanders was always this cranky socialist independent. Both were railing against both Democrats and Republicans. I think part of the attraction is their consistency, because people get tired of politicians who just say whatever you want to hear.

But dig a little bit deeper. When Bernie rails against crony capitalism, or rails against permanent war, or rails against the surveillance state, or the criminal justice system that has packed our prisons, Ron Paul could be giving the same speech. And it's not until the end of the story, when Bernie says: "That's why we need to grow the size of government and give bureaucrats more power," that people hear a difference. That's Bernie's cognitive dissonance: railing against the evils created by too much government power, and then pushing for more government power to solve the problem.

Powell: You're finding a similarity between radical socialists and radical libertarians in identifying problems that young people see. Is it that the young people don't understand the solutions and just identify with the politicians that point out the problems?

Kibbe: Conservatives have this phrase that I don't like at all called "low-information voters." And I don't like it because it's sort of a derogatory term. I think all of us, including me—we're all low-information voters.

There is so much that you don't know, and you can't know, about what the government is doing, about what politicians are really thinking. So, "We the People," to the extent that we pay attention, it's only an inch deep. In practice, you might give a little bit of attention to presidential politics, and if Bernie is railing against the machine, and you're nodding your head yes, like, "Yeah, I get that," you're not so much focused on comparative economic systems, or the type of cost-benefit analysis economists use.

I think if you look at the appeal of Bernie, it's all that anti-establishment "rage against the machine." I think we probably were too optimistic about the Ron Paul movement. We thought it was made up of self-identified libertarians who knew all about property rights and the importance of limiting the power of government. But fast-forward to Rand Paul's run for president in 2016, and Rand lost half of the Ron Paul coalition to Trump. So, raging against the machine could be populist, it could be libertarian, or it could be socialist. I think part of our challenge is to fill in the blanks to show that if you don't like those things contrived and corrupted by Washington power brokers, what you are really saying is, you don't want too much government control over your life.

Lawson: One thing that was striking when we interviewed young people at the big socialist conference in Chicago was how few socialists there were. I'd talk to a random person and ask them, "Why are you a socialist?" And they would say, "I'm for abortion rights." Abortion is an important issue but it's not clear to me how that aligns with socialism. There were people that were there for various environmental concerns, immigration rights, and other "progressive" causes. Somehow, to those attending the conference, all these things came under the banner of socialism. Did you see that at the Ron Paul movement? People identifying as libertarians, but who were there really because they liked guns or smoked weed? Did you see these single-issue people who couldn't broaden their overall philosophy past their primary issue?

Kibbe: There are a bunch of things that a libertarian or conservative coalition would disagree about, but there is a difference between that and the sort of disagreements of the progressive-democratic-socialist coalition. There were core values the Tea Party coalition did agree on: constitutionally limited government, individual freedom, fiscal responsibility. By the way, those ideals in politics are sort of homeless right now. I don't recognize either party pushing for that stuff anymore. Maybe there's an entrepreneurial opportunity there?

The progressive coalition has always been a collection of grievances and identity silos, and they try to check all the boxes, but it is not at all clear that they have a set of common interests that bind them together as a community. So, that's one of the reasons why I'm not so panicked about young people gathering around the banner of socialism. I am not sure that the word "socialism" to them means what you and I think about when we think about government ownership of the means of production.

Powell: It feels like young people are identifying with socialism in a way that they identified with libertarianism a decade ago. How can we turn the tide and show young people the value of liberty, why it should matter to them, and why they should go whole hog on libertarianism and not just on a side issue here or there?

Kibbe: I think we should borrow a page from Ron Paul, Bernie Sanders, and more important, the new "It Girl" in socialist politics, Alexandria Ocasio-Cortez. She had this viral video that sort of created her career. You watch it and she talks about dignity, and she talks about how it is that her opponent is this incumbent-for-life Democrat who's more cozy with Wall Street then he is with "our community." He lives in Washington, he doesn't represent our values, he's all about crony capitalism. He's part of this machine in a faraway place. He's not us. What Ocasio-Cortez believes, at least as represented in this viral video, is something akin to people working together, people cooperating, people trying to solve problems at the community level, from the bottom up. And that, according to her, is how we're going to make the world a better place. And then, at the end, she sneaks her real agenda in: that's why we need Medicare for all, and that's why we need to socialize this, that, and the other thing.

But it's almost an afterthought, it's not a policy or ideological pitch. It's an emotional, populist appeal to people who don't trust the system anymore. And when I hear it at that level, I am like, "Hell yeah, I'm on board." I totally get that it's an emotional appeal, but we can learn from that. What we have to do is rage against the machine. The machine sucks. The machine colludes to help insiders and wealthy corporations game the system against the rest of us. We have that absolutely in common with her. What we have that's different is a beautiful story about cooperation. Remember that whole thing that I just described, about communities working to help one another? That's not socialism, this bottom-up system of tapping into the hopes and dreams of all of us, that's the free market. That, even though I don't like to use the word, is the capitalist system.

Powell: The voluntary system.

Kibbe: The voluntary system. We have to come up with some way to describe what it is we're talking about. Not in terms of the brutal economics of costs and benefits, and supply and demand, but the personal aspirations of people to be free to do cool stuff. Which, by the way, is why I talk about beer so much on my show. Good beer is the product of free-market, entrepreneurial innovation, and it just doesn't happen if people aren't free to choose, and risk, and create, and fail. I use this metaphor because I think people who think beer is cool are probably not going to be reading some of the academic journals that you guys publish in.

Lawson: In fact, that's one reason why we wrote the book. It's because we realized people aren't reading our journal articles. So we figured, we better write something people will read and have fun doing it.

Powell: And leave us all, to paraphrase Milton Friedman, "free to booze."

Kibbe: Free to booze. Free the beer. Beer is freedom. Let's just end it there before we get too boozy. Cheers.

FURTHER READING

We had fun traveling, researching, and writing this book. We hope you enjoyed reading it but we hope you learned something too. Although we tried to write this book in an entertaining style, the subject matter is deadly serious. A misunderstanding of the economic and political consequences of adopting a socialist economic system has ruined millions of lives over the last century, and if similar misunderstandings aren't stamped out today, millions more lives could be ruined.

This book is our small contribution to helping spread a better understanding of the economic, political, and human consequences of socialism. While we tried to play down the social science and history and play up the everyday beer-pricing effects of socialism, some readers may want to explore some of that social science and history for themselves. Here are a few of our recommendations.

Ludwig von Mises launched what became known as the "socialist economic calculation debate" with his essay "Economic Calculation in the Socialist Commonwealth" in 1920. We gave a *very* brief summary of his argument in Chapter Three. His original article is one of the most important economics articles written in the twentieth century and is very readable and freely available online. If you'd like his more complete argument, you can check out his longer book, *Socialism*, that came out a few years later.

Friedrich A. Hayek was Ludwig von Mises's student and he also wrote quite good articles on the socialist calculation debate as well. They are collected in his book *Individualism and Economic Order*. That book is a little tougher reading than Mises's but is still accessible. We also highly recommend Hayek's *Road to Serfdom*. In it, he explains why economic freedom is necessary to have meaningful political freedom. It's a popular press book, and *Reader's Digest* even did a shortened edition of it. We wish all young "democratic" socialists would read it.

Peter Boettke is our favorite economist for understanding how the Soviet Union's economy (dis)functioned. We recommend his *Political Economy of Soviet Socialism* and *Why Perestroika Failed*. They are both academic books but still highly readable.

In Chapter Five, we mentioned Frank Dikötter's *Mao's Great Famine: The History of China's Most Devastating Catastrophe, 1958–1962*. It's excellent. And until the Communist Party's archives in Beijing are fully opened, it's probably the most accurate accounting of the death toll.

Speaking of death tolls, we also recommend *The Black Book of Communism*. It gives a country by country account of the atrocities these regimes committed. We also recommend R. J. Rummel's *Death by Government: Genocide and Mass Murder Since 1900*.

If you search for it, he also has a website with a lot of the information freely available. All of the death tolls involve some speculation and there are different ways different historians classify things, so everyone's numbers differ. But these sources will give you a decent feel for the magnitude of the atrocities that governments, particularly socialist governments, commit.

We mention many books throughout the text. There is no point in listing them all here, but check out the endnotes if you'd like to know more. We'd be remiss, though, not to say something more here about the *Economic Freedom of the World* annual reports that Bob co-authors. We referenced it many times throughout the book. It's the best starting point for examining where on the spectrum between capitalism and socialism any country lies. The reports are freely available online at https://www.fraserinstitute.org/studies/economic-freedom and there is an interactive map as well. You can also look up any of the literally hundreds of academic papers that have used the index and found how greater economic freedom improves lives (or phrased differently, how more socialist countries suck).

We'd recommend a beer book to you, but unlike socialism, consuming the product is better than reading about it. Cheers!

ACKNOWLEDGMENTS

Ben's text message to Bob read, "Have idea for a book. Combines our favorite things. On a plane now. Drinking. Will call later." Thus, our first thanks go to that wonderful combination of two carbons, six hydrogens, and one oxygen atom for fueling Ben's creativity on a long airplane ride. In this way, and many more, without booze this book wouldn't have been possible.

In the course of writing this book, our travel spanned four continents between May 2016 and July 2018. We are in debt to many people for the help they provided in the course of these travels. Li Schoolland, Ian Vasquez, Daniel Raisbeck, Andre Illarionov, Larisa Burakov and Junjie Ma all helped us to make valuable connections in the countries we visited. We thank Julian Villabona and Dean Peng for joining us in our travels and translating for us, as well as keeping us out of any serious trouble while researching the Venezuelan and

Korean chapters. Special thanks to the New Economic School and Paata Sheshelidze and Gia Jandieri for being such great hosts in Georgia and to Gia's aunt for hosting us for a supra. We thank Nataliya Melnyk and the Bendukidze Free Market Center in Kiev for hosting us at their conference and the Unirule Institute for hosting us at their conference in Beijing. We thank José Torra and Marshall Stocker for valuable travel advice and, in Marshall's case, meeting up for drinks in Moscow. Speaking of drinks, thanks to the SMU MBA students who bought us a bunch of shots in Shanghai, and to Cathy, an American Airlines flight attendant, who remembered us from a business class flight to Asia and kept us well lubricated when we were stuck flying proletariat class home from Europe. We benefited from interviews or barroom discussions with scores of people while visiting these countries and are grateful for the insights they provided.

Although we've both written books before, neither one of us had ever tried writing a book like this one. We knew we were capable of addressing a serious topic with insights from economics and history, but we weren't at all confident that we could do that while also integrating firsthand travel experiences and, hopefully, entertaining our readers. So, we traveled to Cuba and wrote it up as a test chapter. We're indebted to a number of our non-academic friends who read early versions of the draft of that chapter and others and provided valuable feedback and, more importantly, encouragement that we were onto something. Thanks to Mat Leger, Jeff Levis, D. J. Deeb, Michael Caplan, Kevin Knox, Michael Hunter, Paul Goins, James Bryan, and Dr. Scott Jones.

Ben also tried out material in public lectures while the manuscript was in various stages of development at the Haverhill Lions Club, Pheasant Ridge Winery, The Infinite Banking Concept, and a seminar for high school students (leaving out some of the drinking stories with this last group), and we thank them for their interest and encouragement to continue with the project.

Ben would also like to acknowledge his dad, Eric, who was an avid reader and drinker. He taught Ben how to drink and socialize in bars. In trying to get our style right for our target audience Ben often thought about whether his dad would have bought this book. Thanks for the help. Cheers!

We also benefited from feedback from our colleagues in the academy. Thanks to the faculty, staff, students, and supporters at the O'Neil Center at SMU and the Free Market Institute at Texas Tech for all of your support while we worked on this project. A special thanks is due in this regard to Daniel Serralde, who accompanied us in Miami and Chicago. We thank seminar participants at the Universidad Francisco Marroquín, the Friedberg Economics Institute, and the American Institute for Economic Research for feedback on the manuscript.

We owe a particularly large debt of gratitude to Peter Boettke and the Mercatus Center at George Mason University. Pete and his colleagues, Mackenzie Robey and Stephanie Haeffele, arranged for about a dozen scholars to read a draft of our manuscript in May 2018 and then spend a day beating us up with suggestions for how to improve the book. It was a valuable and humbling experience. We thank Peter Boettke, Donald Boudreaux, Bryan Caplan, Veronique de Rugy, Brian Doherty, Bobbi Herzberg, Terence Kealey, Matt Kibbe, Tom Palmer, and Sarah Skwire for their participation and feedback. The manuscript was substantially improved in response to their suggestions. Matt and Bryan's suggestion to wrap the book up back in the U.S.A. at the socialist conference was particularly valuable.

We thank Bob's wife, Tracy Lawson, an accomplished author and professional editor, for editing our manuscript, while still managing to let us be our (improper) selves. We also thank Estephania Lujan Padilla for helping to prepare the manuscript for Regnery. Tom Woods and Matt Kibbe provided invaluable advice and assistance in helping us find a home for this book at a popular publisher. We couldn't be more pleased than to have worked with Regnery. We thank Harry Crocker and Kathleen Curran for their careful edits that both improved the manuscript and probably kept us out of trouble for being too offensive.

NOTES

INTRODUCTION

1. James Buchanan, "Economics and Its Scientific Neighbors." In *The Collected Works of James Buchanan Vol. 17 Moral Science and Moral Order* (Indianapolis: Liberty Fund, 2001), 7.
2. Institute of Politics at Harvard University, "Survey of Young Americans' Attitudes toward Politics and Public Service," Harvard University, http://iop.harvard.edu/sites/default/files/content/160423_Harvard%20IOP_Spring%202016_TOPLINE_u.pdf.
3. Bradford Richardson, "Millennials would rather live in socialist or communist nation than under capitalism: Poll," *Washington Times*, November 4, 2017, https://m.washingtontimes.com/

news/2017/nov/4/majority-millennials-want-live-socialist-fascist-o/.

4. "Young Democratic Socialists of America," YDSA, http://www.ydsusa.org/fall_drive.

5. Alex Thompson and Diamond Naga Siu, "Socialism is surging on college campuses," Vice News, October 27, 2017, https://news.vice.com/en_ca/article/mb9p44/socialism-is-surging-on-college-campuses-this-fall.

6. "Red Century," in Opinion Section, *New York Times*, https://www.nytimes.com/column/red-century.

7. "The first Democratic debate: full rush transcript," CBS News, October 13, 2015, https://www.cbsnews.com/news/the-first-democratic-debate-full-rush-transcript/.

8. Joshua Hall and Robert Lawson, "Economic Freedom of the World: An Accounting of the Literature," *Contemporary Economic Policy* 32, no. 1 (2014): 1–19, https://doi.org/10.1111/coep.12010.

9. Johan Norberg, "How Laissez-Faire Made Sweden Rich," Libertarianism.org, October 25, 2013, https://www.libertarianism.org/publications/essays/how-laissez-faire-made-sweden-rich.

CHAPTER ONE

1. We say almost because in 2012 the Center for Participant Education, a student organization at Bob's alma mater, Florida State University, held a program extolling the virtues of

"Democratic North Korea." See https://archive.org/details/ralphieleaks_gmail_CPE5.

2. Valley News Editorial Board, "Close The Gaps: Disparities That Threaten America," Bernie Sanders Senate website, August 5, 2011, https://www.sanders.senate.gov/newsroom/must-read/close-the-gaps-disparities-that-threaten-america.

3. David Sirota, "Hugo Chavez's economic miracle," Salon, March 6, 2013, http://www.salon.com/2013/03/06/hugo_chavezs_economic_miracle/.

4. North Korea and Cuba aren't rated. The latest economic freedom ratings are available online here: https://www.fraserinstitute.org/economic-freedom.

5. Adam Smith, *An Inquiry into the Nature and Causes of the Wealth of Nations* (New York: Modern Library, 1937 [1776]), 423.

6. Sabrina Martin, "Venezuelan Regime Threatens to Expropriate Bakeries, Jeopardizing Bread," PanAm Post, March 13, 2017, https://panampost.com/sabrina-martin/2017/03/13/venezuela-regime-threatens-expropriate-bakeries-jeopardizing-bread/.

7. Tim Worstall, "Congratulations to Bolivarian Socialism: Venezuela is Now The Country with No Beer," *Forbes*, April 30, 2016, https://www.forbes.com/sites/timworstall/2016/04/30/congratulations-to-bolivarian-socialism-venezuela-country-with-no-beer/#53de85c51e53.

8. John Otis, "Venezuela Is Running Out of Beer Amid Severe Economic Crisis," National Public Radio, May 31, 2016, https://www.npr.org/sections/thesalt/2016/05/31/480126445/

venezuela-is-running-out-of-beer-amid-severe-economic-crisis.

9. Vivian Sequera, "Venezuelans report big weight losses in 2017 as hunger hits," *Reuters*, February 21, 2018, https://www.reuters.com/article/us-venezuela-food/venezuelans-report-big-weight-losses-in-2017-as-hunger-hits-idUSKCN1G52HA.

10. Jeffrey Tayler, "Oliver Stone's Disgraceful Tribute to Hugo Chávez," *Foreign Policy*, May 13, 2014, https://foreignpolicy.com/2014/05/13/oliver-stones-disgraceful-tribute-to-hugo-chavez/.

11. Antonio Maria Delgado, "In Venezuela, inflation quadruples to 18,000 percent in two months, with no end in sight," *Miami Herald*, May 2, 2018, http://www.miamiherald.com/news/nation-world/world/americas/venezuela/article210282264.html.

12. William Neuman and Nicholas Casey, "Venezuela Election Won By Maduro Amid Widespread Disillusionment," *New York Times*, May 20, 2018, https://www.nytimes.com/2018/05/20/world/americas/venezuela-election.html.

13. Friedrich Hayek, *The Road to Serfdom* (Chicago: University of Chicago Press, 1944), 69–70.

14. Milton Friedman, *Capitalism and Freedom* (Chicago: University of Chicago Press, 1962), 9.

15. Alexandra Ulmer, "Phone Calls, Dismissal Threats: Venezuela Pressures State Workers to Vote," *Reuters*, https://mobile.reuters.com/article/amp/idUSKBN1AE08P.

CHAPTER TWO

1. Commercial air service to Cuba from the United States was restored on August 31, 2016.

2. Ashley Cowburn, "Cubans Facing Beer Shortage As Thirsty American Tourists Put Island's Main Brewery Under Strain," The Independent, April 10, 2016, https://www.independent.co.uk/news/world/americas/cubans-facing-beer-shortage-as-american-tourist-influx-puts-island-s-main-brewery-under-strain-a6977156.html.

3. While the National Socialists in Germany and the Fascists in Italy were not Marxist socialists, their ideologies were explicitly socialist.

4. Salim Lamrani, "Cuba's Health Care System: A Model For the World," *HuffPost*, August 8, 2014, https://www.huffingtonpost.com/salim-lamrani/cubas-health-care-system-_b_5649968.html.

5. Gilbert Berdine, Vincent Geloso, and Benjamin Powell, "Cuban Longevity: Health Care or Repression?" *Health Policy and Planning* 33, no. 6 (2018): 755–57.

6. Peter T. Leeson, Russell S. Sobel, and Andrea M. Dean, "Comparing the spread of capitalism and democracy," *Economics Letters* 114, no. 1 (2012): 139–41.

CHAPTER THREE

1. Rainer Dormels, "Profiles of the Cities of DPR Korea–Sinuiju," in *North Korea's Cities: Industrial Facilities, Internal Structures and Typification*, Jimoondang, (2014): 119,

https://koreanologie.univie.ac.at/fileadmin/user_upload/p_
koreanologie/North_Korean_Cities/Sinuiju/Sinuiju.pdf.

2. Stephane Courtois, Nicolas Werth, Jean-Louis Panne, Andrzej Paczkowski, Karel Bartosek, Jean-Louis Margolin, *The Black Book of Communism: Crimes, Terror, Repression* (Cambridge: Harvard University Press, 1999), 561.

3. Yeonmi Park, *In Order to Live: A North Korean Girl's Journey to Freedom* (New York: Penguin, 2016).

4. Michael Seth, *A Concise History of Modern Korea: From the Late Nineteenth Century to the Present* (New York: Rowman & Littlefield, 2009), 119.

5. Seth, *A Concise History of Modern Korea*, 119, 121.

6. "Seoul," Wikipedia, https://en.wikipedia.org/wiki/Seoul.

7. "South Korea," World Bank, http://databank.worldbank.org/data/home.aspx.

8. "North Korea," The World Factbook, Central Intelligence Agency, https://www.cia.gov/library/publications/the-world-factbook/geos/kn.html.

9. Park, *In Order to Live*, 129–30.

CHAPTER FOUR

1. Frank Dikötter, *Mao's Great Famine: The History of China's Most Devastating Catastrophe, 1958–1962* (New York: Bloomsbury, 2011), xii–xiii.

2. Matt Kibbe, "China's Socialist God," Free the People, March 19, 2018, https://freethepeople.org/chinas-socialist-god/.

3. Quoted in Dikötter, *Mao's Great Famine*, 70.

4. Bradley Gardner, *China's Great Migration: How the Poor Built a Prosperous Nation* (Oakland: Independent Institute, 2017), 39.

5. Tom Phillips, "The Cultural Revolution: all you need to know about China's political convulsion," *Guardian*, May 10, 2016, https://www.theguardian.com/world/2016/may/11/the-cultural-revolution-50-years-on-all-you-need-to-know-about-chinas-political-convulsion.

6. Valerie Strauss and Daniel Southerl, "How Many Died? New Evidence Suggests Far Higher Numbers for the Victims of Mao Zedong's Era," *Washington Post*, July 17, 1994, https://www.washingtonpost.com/archive/politics/1994/07/17/how-many-died-new-evidence-suggests-far-higher-numbers-for-the-victims-of-mao-zedongs-era/01044df5-03dd-49f4-a453-a033c5287bce/?utm_term=.fc4752f76617.

7. Gardner, *China's Great Migration*, 21, 15.

8. Ibid., 40.

9. Ibid., 2.

10. Jun Mai, "Liberal economics think tank Unirule locked out of its office for 'security reasons' ahead of forum," *South China Morning Post*, May 13, 2017, http://www.scmp.com/news/china/policies-politics/article/2094217/liberal-economics-think-tank-unirule-locked-out-its.

11. Chris Buckley, "In Beijing, Doors Shut on a Bastion of Independent Ideas," *New York Times*, July 11, 2018, https://www.nytimes.com/2018/07/11/world/asia/china-unirule-institute.html#click=https://t.co/aVtzwOKABD.

12. Buckley, "In Beijing, Doors Shut on a Bastion of Independent Ideas."

13. Nectar Gan, "Chinese government pressured property agent into welding iron gates to liberal think tank office doors, penning in workers, director says," *South China Morning Post*, July 12, 2018, https://m.scmp.com/news/china/policies-politics/article/2154872/chinese-liberal-think-tank-blames-government-after?amp=1.

CHAPTER FIVE

1. Courtois et al., *Black Book of Communism*, 78.
2. Ibid., 98.
3. Ibid., 99.
4. Ibid., 102.
5. Ibid., 121.
6. Bryan Caplan, "Lenin the Prohibitionist," The Library of Economics and Liberty, February 14, 2014, http://www.econlib.org/archives/2014/02/lenin_the_prohi.html.
7. S. J. Taylor, *Stalin's Apologist: Walter Duranty: The New York Times's Man in Moscow* (Oxford: Oxford University Press, 1999), 3.
8. Taylor, *Stalin's Apologist*, 175.
9. Ibid., 182.
10. Ibid., 83.
11. Ibid., 163.
12. Ibid.
13. Ibid., 205.

14. Lawrence W. Reed, "A Revolution to Always Remember but Never Celebrate," Foundation for Economic Education, October 16, 2017, https://fee.org/articles/a-revolution-to-always-remember-but-never-celebrate/?utm_source=zapier&utm_medium=facebook.

15. Taylor, *Stalin's Apologist*, 207.

16. Ibid.

17. Ibid., 210, 219.

18. Robert Conquest, *The Harvest of Sorrow: Soviet Collectivization and the Terror-Famine* (New York City: Oxford University Press, 1986), 306.

19. For a concise elaboration of the economic tradeoffs involved in this process see: Bryan Caplan, "Communism," The Library of Economics and Liberty, https://www.econlib.org/library/Enc/Communism.html.

20. To be fair to the column's author, it was the *Times*' editor who picked the title. And the studies the author references looked at women in other socialist countries behind the Iron Curtain, not the Soviet Union. Kirsten R. Ghodsee, "Sources for my New York Times Op-Ed – 'Why Women had Better Sex Under Socialism,'" Harvard University Blog, August 16, 2017, https://scholar.harvard.edu/kristenghodsee/blog/sources-my-new-york-times-op-ed-why-women-had-better-sex-under-socialism.

21. Francine Du Plessix Gray, *Soviet Women: Walking the Tightrope* (New York: Anchor Books, 1990), 34.

22. Du Plessix Gray, *Soviet Women*, 98.

23. Ibid., 20–21.

24. Ibid., 15.
25. Ibid., 14.
26. Ibid., 20.
27. Ibid., 19.
28. Ibid., 17.
29. Ibid., 73.

CHAPTER SIX

1. Much of this discussion is based on a short book I co-authored with Larisa Burakova about the Georgian reforms for the Antigua Forum at the Universidad Francisco Marroquín in Guatemala. See Larisa Burakova and Robert Lawson, *Georgia's Rose Revolution: How One Country Beat the Odds, Transformed Its Economy, and Provided a Model for Reformers Everywhere* (Guatemala: The Antigua Forum, 2013), https://www.amazon.com/Georgia%C2%B4s-Rose-Revolution-Transformed-Everywhere-ebook/dp/B00HUM-MTVO/.

2. http://privatization.ge/?page=4458065d70bc799bc0bdabe4f8 4d379f&ref=y2y2x2v2z2.

3. Kevin Grier, Robert Lawson, and Sam Absher, "You Say You Want a (Rose) Revolution? The Effects of Georgia's 2004 Market Reforms," *Economics of Transition* 27 (2018): 301–323.

CHAPTER SEVEN

1. The Association of Private Enterprise Education, www.apee. org.

2. Frederick Solt, "The Standardized World Income Inequality Database," *Social Science Quarterly* 97 no. 5 (2018): 1267–81. Harvard Dataverse, https://dataverse.harvard.edu/dataset.xhtml? persistentId=hdl:1902.1/11992.

3. Economic Freedom of the World: 2017 Annual Report, https:// www.fraserinstitute.org/studies/economic-freedom-of-the-world-2017-annual-report.

4. ISO Education Department, "Where We Stand: The politics of the International Socialist Organization," International Socialist Organization, https://www.internationalsocialist.org/wp-content/uploads/2017/11/Where_We_Stand.pdf, 1.

5. ISO Education Department, "Where We Stand," 1.

6. Ibid., 1.

7. The pilgrims' experience illustrates the incentive problems on small-scale communes. In 1620, Plymouth Plantation was founded with a system of communal property rights where food and supplies were held in common and distributed based on equality and need. As a result, there were chronic food shortages until 1623, when they created private parcels of land and made families responsible for feeding themselves. Ben wrote up a column based on William Bradford's 1647 history that you can access here: http://www.independent.org/news/article. asp?id=1423.

8. Ana Gonzalez-Barrera and Jens Manuel Krogstad, "What we know about illegal immigration from Mexico," Pew Research

Center, December 3, 2018, http://www.pewresearch.org/fact-tank/2018/12/03/what-we-know-about-illegal-immigration-from-mexico/.

9. Michael Clemens, "Economics and Emigration: Trillion-Dollar Bills on the Sidewalk?" *Journal of Economic Perspectives* 25, no. 3 (2011): 83–106.

10. Benjamin Powell, ed., *Immigration: From Social Science to Public Policy* (New York: Oxford University Press, 2015).

11. Christopher Coyne, *After War: The Political Economy of Exporting Democracy* (California: Stanford University Press, 2008).

12. Robert Higgs, *Crisis and Leviathan: Critical Episodes in the Growth of American Government* (New York: Oxford University Press, 1987).

13. Christopher Coyne and Abigail Hall, *Tyranny Comes Home: The Domestic Fate of U.S. Militarism* (California: Stanford University Press, 2018).

14. Roger Koppl, *Expert Failure* (Cambridge: Cambridge University Press, 2018).

15. Quotes in the following four paragraphs are from Gilad Edelman, "The Socialist Network: Are today's young, Bernie-inspired leftist intellectuals really just New Deal liberals?" *Washington Monthly* July/August 2018, https://washingtonmonthly.com/magazine/july-august-2018/the-socialist-network/.

16. Elizabeth Bruenig, "It's time to give socialism a try," *Washington Post*, March 6, 2018, https://www.washingtonpost.com/opinions/its-time-to-give-socialism-a-try/2018/03/06/c603a1b6-2164-11e8-86f6-54bfff693d2b_story.html?utm_term=.06ef36fc9837.

17. Elizabeth Bruenig, "Let's Have a Good-Faith Argument about Socialism," *Washington Post*, March 11, 2018, https://www. washingtonpost.com/opinions/lets-have-a-good-faith-argument-about-socialism/2018/03/11/96d66720-23e4-11e8-86f6-54bfff693d2b_story.html?utm_term=.ca5990d6e761.

INDEX